Strategic Planning Multitype Library Cooperatives: A Planning Process

ASCLA Changing Horizons Series #2

Nancy M. Bolt
Colorado State Library
201 E. Colfax Avenue
Denver, CO 80203
(303) 866-6733
nbolt@csn.net
(fax) (303) 866-6940

Sandra S. Stephan
Library Consultant
9404 Byeforde Road
Kensington, MD 20895
(301) 933-3234
ss199@umail.umd.edu
(fax) (301) 949-5867

Association of Specialized and Cooperative Library Agencies
American Library Association
Chicago
1998

Cover: Align Design

Printed on 60-pound Arbor Smooth paper, pH-neutral stocks;
bound in 10-point CIS cover stock by Batson Printing Inc.

The paper used in this publication meets the minimum
 requirements of the American National Standard for Information
Sciences--Permanence of Paper for Printer Library Materials,
ANSI Z39.48-1992.

ISBN 0-8389-7926-2

Printed in the United States of America

00 99 98   3 2 1

TABLE OF CONTENTS

WORKSHEETS

EXAMPLES

PREFACE
STRATEGIC PLANNING FOR MULTITYPE LIBRARY COOPERATIVES:
A PLANNING PROCESS

Planning for the Multitype Library Cooperative (MLC) is critical if it is to best assist the library community. Multitype Library Cooperatives are unique organizations in the library community. Unlike local libraries that serve the general or a specific public, MLCs serve as the "libraries' library," providing resources, consultative assistance, continuing education, and other services to librarians. They are often the first and sometimes the last resort of local school, public, academic, and special libraries as these libraries try to improve their service to their clientele.

The Association of Specialized and Cooperative Library Agencies (ASCLA) is the home within the American Library Association for the Interlibrary Cooperation and Networking Section (ICAN). In 1996, ICAN published in ASCLA's *Changing Horizon* series, *Strategic Planning for Library Multitype Cooperatives: Samples and Examples* by Steven Baughman and Elizabeth Curry, a compilation of excerpts from the long range and strategic plans of MLCs. This second in the series, *Strategic Planning for Multitype Library Cooperatives: A Planning Process,* is written as a how-to guide for the MLCs to use as they prepare their plan.

This manual melds conventional long-range planning with more focused strategic planning. This approach acknowledges what an MLC already does and may want to improve AND identifies issues that transcend current services and types of libraries, and that must be dealt with for the MLC to survive and prosper.

The intended audience for this manual is anyone who belongs to, governs, or works in an MLC. This includes MLC directors, governing boards, and staff of member libraries. All participants in an MLC benefit from good planning by the MLC. The manual can be used in its entirety to implement a full scale planning process, or sections of the manual can be used for quick interim planning when necessary (i.e., dealing with a strategic issue that arises).

The authors, Nancy Bolt and Sandy Stephan, have combined library experience of almost 60 years. Both have worked for state library agencies and with MLCs, their members, and staff. They both have extensive experience in planning and evaluation, and have authored numerous articles.

Acknowledgments:

The authors wish to thank Elizabeth Curry and Steven Baughman, who assisted with critiquing drafts of the manual. Early work done by ICAN on a manual was most helpful and parts of that unpublished document are included in this manual. Several other MLC directors also read and provided input on the manual and their help is appreciated.

Thanks also to Bill Wilson, Ethel Himmel, and the committee who wrote the new Public Library Association (PLA) planning process, *Planning for Results*. Their thinking about the planning process influenced us, particularly in the area of measures of success.

Renee Emeson and Kathleen Parent, of the Colorado State Library, assisted with typing, repeated editing, and design work.

Lillian Lewis, of ASCLA, brought the manuscript to print through her management of the publication process.

Finally, the authors survived stimulating, heated, and continuing discussions about the best way to do planning.

HOW TO USE THIS MANUAL

Strategic Planning for Multitype Library Cooperatives: A Planning Process contains:

- Philosophical underpinnings of the process
- Instructions in how to use the process
- Worksheets, exhibits, and examples to help MLC planners use the process
- Two introductory chapters and seven phases as chapters

Worksheets are forms that MLC planners can complete as part of the planning process. They are designed to help planners think through the various steps in planning. They can be copied and used as is or adapted to meet the local MLC situation. These are at the ends of chapters and are lettered alphabetically throughout the manual.

Examples are ideas and formats that the authors composed to show how a part of the planning process might work. These are inserted within and at the ends of chapters and are numbered consecutively throughout the manual.

Exhibits come from actual planning efforts by multitype and public library organizations. Many are included in the first book in this series, *Strategic Planning for Library Multitype Cooperatives: Samples and Examples*. These are found throughout the text.

INTRODUCTION
STRATEGIC & CONVENTIONAL LONG-RANGE PLANNING

*"Long-range planning does not deal with future decisions,
but with the future of present decisions."*
Peter F. Drucker

The benefits of thorough planning, assessment, and evaluation have long been sung in the library arena. The efforts of conducting a planning process have been frequently praised as useful and enlightening. The published plan has not always been implemented as written; nevertheless, plans have been used successfully for political/funding purposes and have indeed served as a guide for library activities. We believe that the readers of this manual know the benefits of planning, that they seek a better understanding of planning that is useful in today's constantly changing environment, and that they want a practical how-to-do-it guide.

The authors kept three objectives in mind in writing the manual for MLCs:
  (1)   Help the MLCs "think out of the box"
  (2)   Help MLCs organize information gathered so it is useful and makes sense
  (3)   Provide a method for making informed and valid decisions about what services
          the MLC will provide

This, the second in the ASCLA *Changing Horizons* series, is a manual on the process of **strategic long range planning**. The manual melds conventional long-range planning with elements of strategic planning. Most planning texts espouse one or the other type of planning or ignore the difference between them. Both strategic thinking, with its environmental focus, and conventional planning, with its analysis of the present, are included in this planning process.

Conventional long range planning has been most widely used in the library field. It is recognized by having goals, objectives, and strategies to be carried out by the organization over a three to five year time frame. It involves analytical decision making and leads planners to re-invent, re-focus and re-organize, based on the current situation.

Strategic planning results in a series or stream of decisions without defining implementation. It involves strategic thinking that pushes us to create the new. It is looking at the critical--or strategic--issues and challenges that the organization faces. Strategic issues usually cross service or constituency lines and must be resolved for the organization to be successful.

The authors believe that the process and resulting plan will be stronger with the combination of the traditional long-range approach and strategic thinking. The strategic part of planning enables rapid change based on a vision of the future, while conventional planning lays out the path to be taken. This planning process, then, gives us direction, acknowledges the present reality, and helps us maintain a control over the inevitable ambiguity caused by the maybes of the future.

The box below compares the two approaches. It shows that strategic planning seeks out critical or strategic issues that challenge the organization; conventional planning looks comprehensively at all services. The organization that thinks strategically is better prepared to take advantage of new opportunities. A defining point for strategic planning is that decisions are based on projecting into the future and looking to the 'outside' environment to define direction. Conventional planning usually deals with updating current services and programs. Strategic planning requires opinion, intuition, 'sensing'; conventional planning appropriately deals with facts and figures. <u>Both</u> are needed to ensure the success of the MLC.

STRATEGIC PLANNING VS.	CONVENTIONAL LONG-RANGE PLANNING
Focuses on the environment	Focuses on the organization
Focuses on strategic issues to move forward	Looks comprehensively at all services
Challenges the status quo	Emphasizes stability
Prepares to take advantage of new opportunities	Follows a blueprint
Predicts, projects, bases decisionson looking from the future	Bases decsions on looking from the present
Anticipates changes	Extrapolates from the past and present
Changes paradigms	Updates current services and programs
Emphasizes opinions, intuition, and the qualitative	Emphasizes facts and the quantitative
Seeks effectiveness, doing the right things	Seeks efficiency, doing things right
Intuitive	Analytical
Art	Science

PLANNING IN GENERAL

Planning is a circular process, it is iterative and relational; it is not linear and cannot be done as one completed step after another. At its most basic, planning can be seen as a circle:

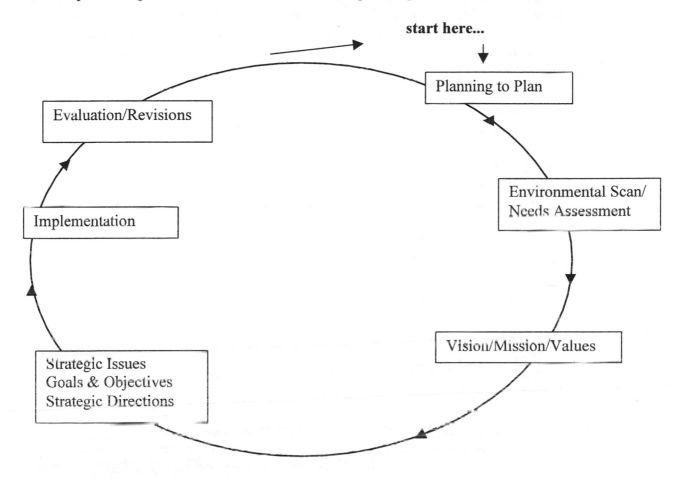

Planning answers **5 key questions:**

Who are our customers?	*Needs assessment*
Where are we/they going?	*Vision, strategic issues & goals*
Where are we now?	*Organization performance & needs*
How will we get there?	*Major strategies and directions*
How will we know when we've arrived?	*Measures of success, objectives & evaluation*

Effective Planning is:
  continuous
  comprehensive
  flexible
  client-centered
  linked to resource allocation
  a process, not a product

PHASES IN THE STRATEGIC PLANNING PROCESS

There are **7 phases in the strategic planning process** used in this manual. As the planning progresses, new data is introduced, alternative methods are selected, and decisions are revised, it is likely that revisions and even repeating parts of steps will be required. Planners and the process must be well prepared, yet absolutely flexible. Allow for and expect changes throughout the development of the plan. Wherever possible, levels of effort are outlined so that each organization can select its own emphasis and resource commitment; however, all the phases should be completed.

I.   Planning to Plan
1. Commitment
2. Purpose
3. Responsibility
4. Planning Team
5. Existing Capabilities
6. Consultants
7. Process, Structure, Level of Effort
8. Resource Requirements
9. Schedule
10. Marketing the Planning Effort

II.   Environmental Scan, Needs Assessment (ESNA)
1. ESNA and Definitions
2. Strategic Issues; Member/Potential Member Needs; Trends
3. Assessment Methods and their Uses

III.   Vision, Mission and Values
1. Vision
2. Mission
3. Values (beliefs, philosophy)

IV.   Analyzing ESNA, Setting Directions, and Measuring Results
1. ESNA Information
2. Strategic Issues
3. Function Areas
4. Goals/Strategic Directions
5. Objectives/Major Strategies/ Measures of Success
6. Rationales

V.   Revisiting Vision and Mission
1. Revise Vision or Goals
2. Finalize Mission

VI.   Implementation of Plan
1. Actions
2. Implementation Time Line
3. Work Plans
4. Reaction
5. Publish and Market
6. Budgeting

VII.   Monitor and Evaluate
1. Celebrate
2. Debrief on the Planning Process
3. Monitor and Evaluate
4. Reassess, Develop Implementation Plan 2

"The shoals are many, but the rewards are great."
Steve Baughman

INTRODUCTION

Multitype Library Cooperatives (MLC) are unique in the library community. They are closer to the individual libraries than state libraries, yet provide services to libraries rather than the public at large. MLCs, by definition, try to meet the needs of more than one type of library and may serve all four--academic, public, school, and special libraries. MLCs face political realities that can be daunting and a planning environment that is more complex than most individual libraries.

DEFINITIONS OF MLCs AND THEIR SERVICES

Definitions

Multitype Library Cooperatives are defined in *Standards for Cooperative Multitype Library Organizations,* published by ASCLA in 1990, as:

> *MULTITYPE LIBRARY ORGANIZATION - a formal cooperative organization that has more than one type (i.e., academic, public, school, and special) of independent and autonomous library or group of libraries working together for their mutual benefit.*

We have chosen to use the term Multitype Library Cooperative. Throughout this workbook we will refer to them as MLCs. In various states, MLCs go by various names. Some MLCs serve multistate geographic areas. They can be designated as:

- regional systems
- regional cooperatives
- regional networks
- regional consortia
- multistate networks

We have also chosen to use the word libraries to designate academic, public, school, and special libraries. When reference is intended to be for only one type of library, it will be specified.

Purpose of MLCs

MLCs typically have one or more of the following main purposes:

- improve local library service
- represent the interests of the member libraries at the state or federal level

5

- enable libraries to share resources
- develop cooperative avenues for libraries to work together
- advocate for support of member libraries at the local, state, or federal level.

Organization of MLCs

MLCs serve the needs of their members. Membership can be based on several models, often tied to how the MLC is funded. Models can include any of the following factors:

- libraries can join only an MLC that serves their geographic area
- libraries can join any MLC that has services they need and choose
- a limited number of types of libraries may be served (i.e., only public and academic)
- there may be full members and associate members with limited services
- MLC costs may be paid by a combination of state, federal, and/or local funds
- MLCs may charge a membership fee for all services
- MLCs may offer some services for free to all members, but charge for other services
- governance may be by member librarians
- governance may be by lay representatives from member governing boards
- governance may be by the state library
- governance may be by a combination of the above

While any of the above factors may be a part of an MLC organization, they all serve more than one type of library and that members determine the types of services that are provided. Sometimes this is delegated to the MLC board and sometimes decided by the membership as a whole.

MLCs may be created in state law or by the state library, or by libraries in a geographic area deciding to come together to facilitate joint projects or services. However they are created, MLCs typically are required to plan, budget, and report to members, the MLC board, the state library, or some other funding authority.

Services Offered by an MLC

MLCs offer the following types of services, although all services listed below may not be offered by all MLCs. There may also be other services that MLCs provide.

- consulting or technical assistance
- continuing education
- cataloging
- electronic networking
- interlibrary loan
- reciprocal borrowing
- publications and newsletters
- building and space planning
- group purchases
- cooperative collection development
- cooperative programming
- database management
- delivery/courier system
- video cooperatives

6

- circulating collections
- bookmobiles
- Web pages
- electronic mail/list servs
- planning
- facilitation of meetings
- financial accounting
- advocacy/expert testimony
- lobbying
- public relations/marketing
- Free-nets
- backup reference
- shared personnel
- technical services
- union lists

- grant writing
- graphics
- policy development
- personnel consultation
- meeting/conference planning
- preservation facilities/advice
- professional collection
- program evaluation
- board training
- research and development
- retrospective conversion
- shared licensing
- software development
- fax network
- group access catalogs (GAC)

MLC staff often say they provide "anything the members want and the board decides to offer." This implies a planning process that determines what the members or their end users want, a process for the board to decide what services the MLC should provide, and the identification of the resources needed to provide the service.

Role of MLCs in the Library Community

MLCs play a vital role in the library community. They are often the closest contact a library can reach when it faces a problem, needs assistance or guidance, or needs services it doesn't want to hire staff to do. In many rural areas, libraries may be directed by people without formal training in library service. For them, the majority of their library skills and knowledge may be provided by consultation and staff development from the MLC.

MLCs draw together different types of libraries for communication, personal networking, idea sharing, joint planning, continuing education, and economies of scale. They provide a critical link among local libraries. They also serve as a link between their members and the state library and/or state government. MLC staff often represent member interests on statewide library, education, or government committees, and advocate for libraries and members to receive services, be included in projects, or receive recognition.

MLCs may be required to submit annual plans and/or reports to the state library. They must prepare budgets, plans, and reports for their own governing boards. Most MLCs consider the needs of their member libraries primarily in their planning and delivery of services. Most MLCs, however, also look at the relationship of their members' needs to the needs of other libraries and MLCs around the state. Needs of libraries throughout a state often overlap and a MLC can make more effecient and effective use of its own resources by cooperating with other MLCs and with the state library.

POLITICAL REALTIES FOR MLCs

Meeting Multiple Needs

MLC directors typically report to a board composed of member representation. They must listen to and consider the interests of all types of member libraries and all sizes of libraries, some of which may be very different. The MLC director must be able to find commonalities among these various needs and not neglect any one type of library. Multistate MLCs must strive to meet the needs, not only of different types of libraries, but also of different states.

In addition, some types of libraries are easier to serve than others, and some need more services than others. Large public, academic, or school libraries may need less direct consultation or continuing education, but rely more on the MLC for electronic networking. Libraries not directed by a professional librarian may rely heavily on the MLC staff for consultation and "hand holding" as basic decisions about library services are made. The MLC director may be asked to intervene in personnel decisions that pit a local library director against his/her governing authority. It may be "easier" to serve public libraries, where the decision making process is in an independent library board, than school libraries where there may be a school principal or superintendent who is hostile and/or non-supportive of school libraries. There can also be conflicts over the demand on resources from different types of libraries or competition between the MLC and one or more of its members for money (i.e., fund-raising, state aid) or other resources.

Multiple Bosses

Many MLCs must take into consideration multiple "bosses." While there may be a governing board, the MLC may also have reporting and statutory requirements from the state library or state government. In addition, MLC staff may be caught between board members and THEIR supervisory authority, particularly where funding comes from membership dues. The MLC is faced with meeting the needs of members, the board, and state legal authorities.

Future vs. Present

MLC staff are also torn between the need to continue trusted and used member services AND the need to look to the future for needs local libraries may not yet even recognize. This can present a problem for planning and is why this manual seeks to combine intuitive and targeted strategic planning with analytical and comprehensive long-range planning. Because current services are often so popular, needs assessments of members often confirm the status quo of MLC services. It is easy for an MLC to get bogged down in current products and services and how to update them for the future rather than challenging the status quo and looking toward a different future. Later in this manual, the authors present ways to conduct a needs assessment to ascertain members' needs and wants for services and how to conduct an environmental scan to determine trends and issues outside the MLC that will impact its future.

MLC staff, because of their frequent involvment in state and national activities, are in a position to see future trends and issues, and help their member libraries be prepared to address them. MLC staff must also look at the needs of the populations served by member libraries, of broader societal needs, and help member libraries be prepared to address these needs as well.

A good MLC planning process will strive to combine and intertwine future trends and current needs. It will plan for members to continue to receive services they rely on and still push members to see the need for totally new approaches to old problems and new ways to address new needs. Most MLC plans are finally approved by the board and possibly by the full MLC membership. The plan must reassure the MLC members that favorite and popular services will remain, and also show and convince members that the MLC board and staff are looking toward the future and new challenges that will be presented.

> *The plan must reassure the MLC members that favorite and popular services will remain, and show that staff are looking toward the future and new challenges.*

Visibility

MLCs are in a contradictory position in obtaining recognition for their work and services. An MLC's services are often transparent to the library user, and credit for success goes to the local library, not the MLC. While this certainly benefits libraries, it can lead to a lack of understanding and possibly support by funding authorities who may not recognize the extent and value of the service provided by the MLC. When it is time to seek support for continued or increased MLC funding, particularly if this is provided by a legislative authority, the MLC must often rely on member libraries to advocate because library users are not aware of the role the MLC plays in the delivery of quality service.

Cooperation and Partnerships

To a greater extent than any individual local library, MLC success depends on its ability to build partnerships and cooperative relationships.

Many MLCs develop new services through member committees composed of like or different type libraries. In either case, the various situations and needs of member libraries must be considered, and it is often the MLC staff who facilitate this process through problem solving, consensus building, and decision making. Likewise, the MLC is in position to represent the needs of members and build partnerships with local educational agencies, non-profits, government, and business, on behalf of all or some member libraries. This can extend the reach and recognition of library services to a larger and influential stakeholder community.

At a broader geographic level, MLCs can seek partnerships with other MLCs, the state library, and statewide groups to further the interests of member libraries and libraries in general. One MLC can even take the lead for a statewide project. Multistate networks can seek partnerships across state lines for programs and projects. MLC staff cannot succeed without the collaborative support of member libraries, and no MLC can be truly successful without developing broad partnerships within and outside the library community.

PLANNING IS CRITICAL FOR MLCS

MLCs in a Time of Rapid Change

The rapid changes in technology, finances, and political actions also make it imperative that MLCs engage in planning. It can be a matter of survival as other organizations compete for resources and recognition. The information needs of our society are changing rapidly, thus also the demands on local libraries. The MLCs typically have less local bureaucracy and can respond more rapidly to the demands on and needs of local libraries. Decisions about new services, new programs, and redirected budgets can typically be made by a local governing board much faster than similar actions at the state library level.

This quick turn-around ability means that MLC staff and boards must always be aware of new issues that arise in the broader library community and be able to relate these issues back to their member libraries. They can look toward the future and prepare local libraries for societal changes that are on the way. In recent years, MLCs have seen a revolution in the types of services needed by their members, particularly in the area of electronic networking. Some services may no longer be needed and can be replaced with new services as libraries respond to the changing demands of their users.

Importance of Planning

The unique organizational and governmental nature of MLCs, their relative independence, their role in the library community, and the political realities they face all make planning critical for an MLC. Having clear goals allows "informed opportunism," i.e., taking advantage of opportunities that arise. The quick response ability allows new needs of members to be met, strategic issues to be addressed, and new trends to be incorporated into the MLC's services.

MLCs as decentralized organizations are better positioned than traditional public bureaucracies to respond quickly to changing circumstances and needs at the grassroots level. MLC horizontal structure and project teamwork is at the core of the latest management tomes. Without strategic planning, however, an MLC service program can be based on equal portions of serendipity, sentimentality, drift, and inertia. A grab bag of programs and services based on things somebody wants, things nobody else is doing, things always done, things for which grant money is available, and things others are doing but would just as soon push off on someone else, leaves an organization vulnerable to ineffective use of resources and increasing irrelevance.

These same factors that make planning so essential can also contribute a resistance to planning because "things change too quickly to plan." More so than for other agencies, MLCs must plan in a clear, direct, yet flexible manner. It is the authors hope that this manual will help that occur.

WHAT IS IT?

It's pre-planning, organizing the planning process. Guiding decisions and a planning outline are shaped by these questions: How are we going to plan? What process will we use? What will it include? Who's going to be involved? How much effort and resources will we commit?

WHY DO IT?

Any project undertaken must be thought through first. Thinking through the complete planning process and answering important questions initially will save time and money and help ensure a smooth running project at the outset.

STEPS

1. Commit to planning
2. Define purpose and scope of plan
3. Assign responsibility
4. Select planning team
5. Evaluate existing capabilities
6. Use consultants?

7. Outline the process, structure, and level of effort
8. Determine resource requirements
9. Decide on schedule
10. Market the planning effort

KEY IDEAS & CONCEPTS

- Clearly define the reason and parameters for the plan
- Be as inclusive as possible, but limit the number of people for decision making
- Lay out the time and dollars anticipated for the project....then add more
- Get outside help
- "Sell" the planning effort throughout the process

WORKSHEETS (at the end of chapter)

Worksheet A: Purpose/Scope, Time Frame, Responsibilities
Worksheet B: Planning Team Charge
Worksheet C: Knowledge & Skills Needed for Planning
Worksheet D: Outline and Schedule
Worksheet E: Level of Effort
Worksheet F: Estimating Expenses
Worksheet G: Planning Budget
Worksheet H: Marketing the Effort

PLANNING PROCESS

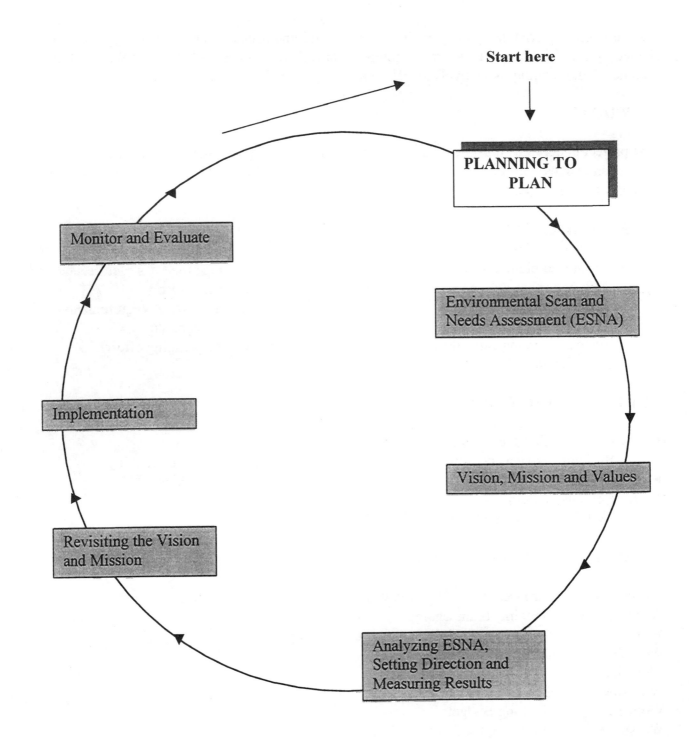

Start here

PLANNING TO
PLAN

Environmental Scan and
Needs Assessment (ESNA)

Vision, Mission and Values

Analyzing ESNA,
Setting Direction and
Measuring Results

Revisiting the Vision
and Mission

Implementation

Monitor and Evaluate

"Whether you believe you can do a thing or not, you are right."
Henry Ford

There are ten steps an MLC must go through to prepare for the planning process. Without thorough preparation for planning, an effective planning process cannot be conducted.

STEP 1. COMMIT TO PLANNING

The need to develop a long-range plan may emanate from anyone or any group involved with the MLC. Once the idea takes on momentum, the system director, the policy board, advisory groups, and management staff must commit to planning. Commitment means making the process a top priority for eight to twelve months--not just squeezing it in between other number one projects. It means assigning staff and appropriating adequate resources. There must be key decision makers and leaders who champion the process and who believe that following the process will bring good answers even if there are surprises. Successful MLCs have highly respected directors who are frequently the initiators of and champions for developing the plan. Finally, commitment means that all authorities agree to implement the approved strategic long-range plan.

STEP 2. DEFINE PURPOSE AND SCOPE

Articulating the specific reasons for planning for your organization provides the parameters for the process and tells people what the MLC is about. A plan may be needed if:
- it is required by the state
- there is a major initiative the MLC is undertaking
- member libraries are facing new challenges and therefore making demands for new services
- the MLC seeks new thinking and renewal, possibly reorganization
- there is an increase or decrease in funds
- there is a new executive director

Once the purpose for planning is clear, define the scope of the plan. The scope indicates whether this is for the MLC as a whole, or a service area such as reference. The MLC could also be writing a plan for all the libraries in the cooperative. Clearly stating the purpose and scope in just a few sentences gives the "why and for what" the MLC has for planning. If there are one or two major issues the board and director want the plan to address, they should be included in the purpose and scope. *Worksheet A, Purpose/Scope, Time Frame, Responsibilities* allows the planners to develop the purpose and scope of the planning effort.

STEP 3. ASSIGN RESPONSIBILITY

Planning is a function of the MLC board that is frequently assigned to the director and staff to

13

carry out with board member involvement and always with final board approval of the plan. Sometimes, a planning team of the board takes responsibility and the director serves as staff to the board. Whatever the circumstances, the MLC director must be intimately involved in the planning and may choose to lead the process. The director could also delegate the responsibility to a staff member to serve as plan coordinator. In many MLCs, the director and staff are expected to run the operation, make the decisions, and do the planning with periodic input from the board. In these cases, the director and staff may be responsible for drafting much of the strategic plan. It does not preclude, however, the broad involvement of members and the input and reaction from the board and key stakeholders. Whatever the decision on "who plans," make it up front. If much data are being collected, a data coordinator should also be appointed.

There is also a broader responsibility for the plan that includes all those affected; MLC and member library staff participation is critical. Not only will actual implementation rely on MLC and member library staffs, but their involvement generates a greater commitment to the process. It really is true--"the greater the participation, the greater the buy-in." Staff from member libraries and the MLC can work on task teams that gather data and conduct research on critical issues and targeted services. Continually seek comments and input. Regular communication to all members and staff about progress and the proposed content of the plan is also essential and is discussed in more detail in *Marketing the Planning Effort, Step 10.* Assign responsibility for planning tasks in *Worksheet A, Purpose/Scope, Time Frame, Responsibilities.*

STEP 4. SELECT PLANNING TEAM

A core group of people to steer the process is the best method for developing the plan. This group works through the structure, sets the calendar, and makes preliminary decisions on what

goes into the plan. It may be useful to conduct some training and have readings on planning and group decision making as the team organizes and as each phase begins. Planning team orientation cannot be haphazard. The 1998 PLA *Planning for Results: A Library Transformation Kit* devotes several pages to training the team. Background readings on the MLC, on futurist predictions, articles on library trends and futures, examples of other state and system plans, planning methods and process, working as a team, and group decision making are all potential areas to cover with the planning team.

> *A core group of people to steer the process is the best method for developing the plan.*

While it is the board that appoints the team and approves the charge, it is the director's or planning coordinator's job to articulate the charge and even negotiate the responsibilities with the planning team. *Example 1, Charge to Planning Team,* shows:

Planning to Plan	CHARGE TO PLANNING TEAM	Example 1

1. Analyze the current and future environment for library services, the current strengths and weaknesses of the MLC, and identify member needs for MLC services.
2. Create a vision to lead the MLC and members into the next decade and articulate the MLC's mission for the next three years
3. Ensure an inclusive process with wide participation.
4. Develop a strategic plan for the MLC that provides broad direction and clear prioritization for MLC services through goals or goal areas, outcome objectives, and recommended major strategies.
5. Report at least twice during the process and present the final plan for approval and implementation to the MLC Board.

The smallest of planning teams or steering committees are made up of the MLC director, the plan coordinator (if there is one), and one or two representatives from the board. A more inclusive team would have selected representatives from among the different types and sizes of member libraries, advisory groups, key MLC management staff, and even an administrator from a non-member library or the state library. The planning team should mirror the composition of the MLC membership. Planners must represent the various values and perspectives of the membership. Use *Worksheet B, Planning Team Charge,* to draft a charge and list potential members of the planning team.

Planning to Plan	Excerpt PLANNING TEAM		Worksheet B
Planning Team Charge:			
Planning Team Members: Name	Phone	Assigned to call	Agreed to serve

Careful consideration of the makeup of the team is very important. A good working group numbers between 9 and 12; less may be appropriate for a small system, more is unwieldy and makes it difficult to reach consensus. If a really large group is required politically, make it a planning advisory committee and keep the decisions at a steering committee level.

Certainly the wider the participation in the process the more buy-in there will be for implementing the plan. Including both members and non-members for input and feedback is important. Consider asking representatives to serve on the planning team, on a constituent advisory committee, or task forces--this creates the commitment to succeed.

In the process recommended in this manual, environmental scan and needs assessment (ESNA) plays a large role. ESNA teams can be formed and charged with gathering information in specific topic areas or implementing a specific environmental scan or needs assessment method.

An inclusive and participative process provides breadth and depth to the identification of needs and issues. Wide participation leads to greater acceptance and success. Having a planning advisory committee or client reaction group is one way to ensure thoughtful input and discussion of issues without compromising the effectiveness of the planning team. This is also a solution for being inclusive without jeopardizing control over the direction for the MLC when there is discord or there are widely divergent views for future services. Such a group could meet a few times to provide vision, input on needs, and reaction to the draft plan. It would be most useful if this group could get input from its various constituencies. When meeting is not feasible, written or electronic communication and reaction still benefit the process.

In this planning manual, it is the planning team that does the job. There is one other important item to consider--who chairs the team? While the MLC director is integrally involved in the process, he/she must guard against dominating it and should choose not to head the group that steers the effort. A board member or influential, skilled administrator from a member library might be a more appropriate chair. A key stakeholder from the larger library community or from among community partners might be asked to chair the team, thus giving the process and resulting plan increased objectivity and perhaps more credibility within the MLC community. The level of responsibility for chairing the team can vary greatly. The chair takes on greater significance when there are fewer planners and the influence and leadership is centralized. When there is a plan coordinator, the chair is more of a conductor of meetings and a mover of the process, leaving the logistics, and the "doing" to the coordinator. On many occasions, the chair may be a convener giving the reigns over to the consultant or a discussion facilitator.

Example 2, Main Players' Responsibilities Chart, lists many of the duties of the main players in the process. While not exhaustive, it should help distinguish the roles and show the many possibilities available. The chair may have a lot of power or may have a more equal role to the members. Whether the MLC director serves as plan coordinator, appoints a coordinator, or serves as staff to a board that becomes the planning team, he/she usually remains the overall manager of the effort. It is, after all, the MLC's plan and the director is hired to run the MLC. A further caution to directors is to be as clear as possible during planning discussions as to when the director's hat is on, i.e., when a management decision is being made, and when he/she is an equal member of the group--especially if it is a staff or staff and member team.

Planning to Plan		MAIN PLAYERS' RESPONSIBILITIES CHART		Example 2
MLC BOARD	MLC DIRECTOR	PLAN COORDINATOR	DATA COORDINATOR	PLANNING TEAM
Determines purpose and scope Approves planning process and budget Appoints planning team (PT) Oversees planning process Approves vision, mission, values Approves plan Helps market process and plan Oversees implementation	Sells board on planning Prepares planning budget with plan coordinator (PC) With board, determines purpose and scope Manages overall planning process Serves as member of planning team Is plan coordinator or works with PC May help write plan Manages marketing of process and plan Presents plan for approval to board Manages implementation	With director, prepares planning budget With director, plans PT meetings Works with consultant or facilitators "Educates" the PT Manages all logistics e.g., meetings, retreats Sees to all supplies Acts as staff to PT e.g., prepares worksheets, provides reports, takes notes, trouble shoots Writes newsletter or oversees Coordinates ESNA and ESNA teams or works with data coordinator With director, sees to marketing of process and plan Writes plan or oversees (or works with) consultant writing plan	Manages ESNA, works with or under plan coordinator Conducts all or parts of ESNA Works with consultant Synthesizes data, information, reports for presenting to PT	Chair conducts meetings or passes to consultant or facilitator as appropriate Team is educated about the MLC and planning Appoints and charges ESNA teams Makes decisions and recommendations Provides content for plan Helps market process and plan

STEP 5. EVALUATE EXISTING CAPABILITIES

Think about the available knowledge and experience--that of MLC and member library staffs--that can be used in this strategic long-range planning effort. Consider these possibilities:

- board members experienced in the process
- time the MLC director can dedicate to organizing and actually writing the plan
- freeing up a staff member to be plan coordinator
- clerical support for meetings, for compiling the plan
- publishing the plan in-house
- success in designing and conducting surveys, conducting focus groups, and other means of getting considered, constructive input
- an objective outsider

Now use *Worksheet C, Knowledge and Skills Needed for Planning*, to evaluate the knowledge and skills needed and who might have them. What else might make the process stronger? Would having a designated, objective facilitator help the team work through issues and allow for full participation in discussion? Can that expertise be borrowed from the community or the state library agency ? Or is best to hire a consultant?

STEP 6. USE CONSULTANTS?

Consultants come in many flavors and can be contracted to do one part of the process or facilitate the entire process. As the planning team outlines the structure and activities for developing the plan, the need for consultant expertise and facilitation will become evident. A word of caution here: it may be tempting to have someone "just write the plan" but it will be useless to the organization without going through the all-important **process** of planning and consensus decision making.

Typically, one or more consultants are used to conduct vision and mission writing retreats or weekend retreats where much of the heart of the plan is drafted. They also are most helpful in conducting focus groups and stakeholder interviews to ensure anonymity and honest feedback that might not be

> *Hiring a consultant with expertise to facilitate the entire process and guide the actual writing of the plan is ideal. Planners can be totally involved in debate and not burdened with methodology.*

attained with staff. Here is where state library agency consultant staff could be useful, as well as with other short term interventions. Check with library development staff at the state library agency and ask what and how much they can do. They may not have the expertise, but ask whether there is money available to conduct a statistically sound telephone survey, hire a consultant, provide training for the planning team, etc.

Hiring a consultant with expertise in strategic or long range planning to facilitate the entire process and guide the writing of the plan is ideal. This way planners can be totally involved in debate of crucial issues and decisions and not be doubly burdened with methodology for processes to be used and seeing that all the steps are adequately covered. MLC directors experienced in planning say that a consultant is especially needed for *Setting Direction, Phase IV*, where all the data gathered is turned into goals or strategic directions--an intuitive, facilitative process that can be overwhelming to those vested in the outcome. To successfully facilitate the setting of directions, the consultant must have been part of the process up to this point. Having a planning consultant for the whole process does not preclude using volunteer expertise and state library development consultants who can be very helpful during parts of the process or as part of the planning team.

Using consultants has its pluses and minuses. Consider making a plus and minus list for the MLC's specific situation. See if some of these apply:

Consultants	
+Plus	**-Minus**
+ planners/staff can totally focus on content	- consultant could interfere
+ consultant has tools and techniques that help	- too much process can cause delay
+ consultant is skilled in facilitation	- staff don't gain experience in
+ consultant's time is dedicated to the one job	planning facilitation
+ staff can continue to do their regular jobs	- consultant's bias may obstruct
	- costs are in real dollars

Finding the right consultant(s) is very important, as the plus and minus columns imply. Not only should the consultant be experienced and have good references, he/she should "fit" with the working style of the MLC and the planning team. It is best to send out a request for proposal (RFP) to obtain a good field of consultants to select from; there is no problem in sending to targeted individuals as long as each applicant has equal opportunity. Some organizations can hire consultants with letters of agreement, others may want to have or be required to have a more official contract. Planning consultants are usually contracted for the project with a set amount of dollars; however, hourly contracts are also done. The authors openly acknowledge that in a fixed-fee contract they put in more of their own time than they get paid for in order to do a conscientious job and stay within the project budget. It is possible that extra funds can become available or other line item accounts can be used for small add-on projects that crop up (e.g., making an unscheduled presentation that comes out of the training budget).

STEP 7. OUTLINE THE PROCESS, THE PLAN, AND LEVEL OF EFFORT

At this step, the thoughts and decisions made about how the planning will take place and what the plan will look like are written down. Two outlines are called for: one is an outline of the process to be used in developing the plan and the second is a preliminary draft of what the plan itself will include. As the outlines are developed, options available to the MLC and the level of effort for each major activity are determined.

Outline of the Process

Making decisions during the planning-to-plan phase begins the development of an outline of the process. The outline covers the major activities, who is to accomplish them, and who is to lead. Later, in the scheduling step, dates will be added. *Example 3, Planning Process Outline*, shows how a process might be organized:

Planning to Plan	PLANNING PROCESS OUTLINE	Example 3
ACTIVITY	**WHO'S INVOLVED**	**WHO LEADS**
1. Kick Off Meeting: presentation by a futurist, a review of the planning process	MLC staff and members	Planning team (PT) chair, MLC director, board member, plan coordinator, or consultant
2. Background Readings/Training	Planning team and key players	Plan coordinator
3. Planning Newsletter: first edition disseminated, timetable and content for future issues determined	MLC, board, member libraries--extra copies for wider distribution	Plan coordinator or editor
4. Planning Team (PT) Meetings: schedule and plan tentative content for each meeting; in first or second, identify data gaps and assign ESNA Teams (see #6)	Planning team, steering committee if have one	PT chair, MLC director, or facilitator/consultant
5. ESNA - Environmental Scan and Needs Assessment: results of data gathering underway in anticipation of process is reported to PT; data gathering continues with reports to PT	Planning team, board, MLC senior management staff and selected member representatives	Facilitator/consultant
6. Vision/Mission Meeting takes place while ESNA is being conducted.	Planning team, plan coordinator, and ESNA teams	Data coordinator
7. ESNA Teams: work on assigned data gathering tasks, report to PT.	Planning team, plan coordinator, data coordinator	ESNA teams
8. Planning Retreat: Set Directions (Strategic Directions/Goals and Objectives) and Measures of Success	Planning team, MLC key staff	Plan coordinator or facilitator/consultant
9. Member Review of Goals and Directions: through written input, e-mail, and area open meetings	MLC and member staffs	Plan coordinator or consultant
10. Revisit Vision, Mission and Revise Goals and Directions: and incorporate other input	Planning team	MLC director, plan coordinator, or facilitator/consultant
11. Implementation Meeting: to develop the activities that carry out the major strategies--get ideas and first year activities	MLC staff, selected representatives/managers from member libraries, ESNA team chairs, planning team	PT chair or MLC director
12. Review Final Draft of Plan: available for comment and one open meeting to resolve differences (if needed)	MLC staff, member libraries, key stakeholders, planning team	PT chair, MLC director, or plan coordinator
13. Plan Approval	MLC board	PT chair and MLC director

Planning to Plan	PLANNING PROCESS OUTLINE	Example 3 cont.
14. Publish Plan: send out final copy with photographs to printer, disseminate	MLC staff, board, member libraries, key stakeholders, other cooperatives in state...	Plan coordinator
15. Celebration and Evaluation: thank you's to all involved in the process, evaluate the effort. Evaluation of the plan and progress toward the goals is ongoing; review every 3 to 6 months and formally once a year or when the next implementation plan is written	Planning team, board, MLC staff, ESNA teams, other involved in planning effort	MLC Director or board chair

Use *Worksheet D, Outline and Schedule*, to outline and schedule the planning process.

Planning to Plan	Excerpt OUTLINE AND SCHEDULE		Worksheet D
Planning Activity	Who's Involved	Who Leads	Date

Draft Plan Outline

In this pre-planning stage it is useful to delineate what the planning team thinks the final plan should include. A perusal of other system, state, or organization plans will help the group see potential models and make tentative decisions on the components they prefer. The first book in the ASCLA *Changing Horizons* series, *Strategic Planning for Library Multitype Cooperatives: Samples and Examples,* shows plan outlines in the form of tables of contents for nine cooperatives, systems, or state libraries. An outline for the strategic long-range planning format used in this manual might look something like *Example 4, Strategic Long-Range Planning Format.*

Planning to Plan	STRATEGIC LONG-RANGE PLANNING FORMAT	Example 4
Preface--very brief overview of the planning process and thank you's. **Executive Summary**--of strategic issues, function areas, goals/strategic directions, objectives/major strategies and major activities **Vision, Mission, Values** **Setting Direction and Measuring Results**-- **Strategic Issues,** the critical challenges facing the MLC **Functions,** the categories selected as MLC functions **Goals/Strategic Directions,** the broader statements of what is to be achieved under the function **Strategic Directions,** the more specific targets that will move the MLC toward its goals **OR** **Measurable Objectives,** specific measurable targets **Rationales,** the reasons for selecting the course of action **Measures of Success,** how the MLC will know it has been successful **Implementation and Evaluation**--description of how the plan will be implemented including who will be involved and how the evaluation process will be used **Appendices**--profile of the MLC, charts/graphs on demographics, data gathered		

Level of Effort

> *The more the levels of effort are determined in the planning-to-plan phase, the closer the process will be to budget projections and time schedule-- and the more it will spare staff frustrations while meeting board expectations.*

There are many options or levels of effort the MLC can undertake within each phase of the planning process. The more the levels of effort are determined in the planning-to-plan phase, the closer the process will be to budget projections and time schedule--and to spare staff frustrations while meeting board expectations.

The levels of effort can be seen as a continuum from a basic level to an extensive level of time and resources. The basic and extensive levels are briefly described for six areas with examples of varying effort that could take place along the continuum. The MLC director, with the board, are best able to decide where on the continuum their effort can best succeed. *Example 5, Level of Effort*, shows what this continuum would be for each step in the planning process.

Levels can change for each area of effort undertaken. If resources are scarce, funds might be conserved by choosing the basic level on some steps and the extensive level on other steps.

Area of Effort	Basic Level		Extensive
WHO PLANS	MLC Director 1 staff, 1 board member	. . . add members. . .	18 members on planning committee, 6 member steering committee, task teams and member meetings
EXPERTISE NEEDED	MLC only . . . from members . . . from community . . Consultant for whole process		
MARKETING the PLAN	Periodic memos, reports at regular meetings Notice of published plan	. . . regular updates . . . . . . distribute plan. . .	Discuss at unit meetings, at specially held planning meetings of members. Publicize widely, distribute plan, make visits/presentations
ENVIRONMENTAL SCAN NEEDS ASSESSMENT	Use available reports, statistics, member plans local knowledge	. . . quick surveys . . .	Focus groups, town SCAN, meetings, members vision interviews
VISION, MISSION, VALUES	MLC Director . . . Planning Team . . . MLC staff. . . Member representatives, key and Board		stakeholders
SETTING DIRECTION	MLC Director	. . . plus staff . . . Planning Team . . .	ESNA teams, member representatives, key stakeholders
IMPLEMENT-ATION	MLC Director and 1 or 2 staff write action plan	. . . MLC staff . . .	MLC staff and members participate. Evaluate alternative activities against set criteria and select best actions
MONITORING/ EVALUATING	Select limited areas to collect data and evaluate Subjective evaluation	. . . survey customers . . .	Ongoing customer surveys, target key services for outcome measures, and evaluate major activities Update the plan

Worksheet E, Level of Effort is for the MLC specific planning effort.

Planning to Plan		Excerpt	Worksheet E
		LEVEL OF EFFORT	
Areas of Effort	Basic	Middle ground	Extensive

STEP 8. DETERMINE RESOURCE REQUIREMENTS

Obtaining needed financial resources to conduct the effort is essential; it may be taken care of in the general budget, or specific funding may be sought. In a larger organization it may well be a part of the budget since it will be a relatively minor expenditure in comparison with the overall budget. In the smaller MLC, however, a special allocation may be needed. If it is difficult to obtain the needed funding to develop the plan, consider establishing a time frame that takes in two budget cycles. Funds might also be available through special grants or from the state library. An estimate of the amount of funding needed will be based on the process and plan desired and the levels of effort selected. One thing for certain, the MLC and board must be able to justify the activities in the planning process right up to and including publishing the finished product-- especially if a glossy publication with photographs is desired.

> *Perhaps the more important, and often scarcer resources needed are the involvement and the time of staff and key decision makers.*

Perhaps the more important and often scarcer resources needed are the involvement and the time of staff and key decision makers. The planning team must be prepared to put in the time--an average of one day a month for ten to twelve months, plus some homework, sub-committee work, full day retreats, and member/staff meetings. Add days for the MLC director, planning coordinator and other primary staff. If a consultant is hired for the project, 3 or 4 one- and two-day meetings/retreats might be more practical and perhaps less time consuming for the planning team. In the words of John Bryson, author of *Strategic Planning for Public and Nonprofit Organizations* (p.56),"If there is not enough time for everything, then something else--not strategic planning--should go." Use *Worksheet F, Estimating Expenses*, and *Worksheet G, Planning Budget*, to develop a proposed and final budget for the planning process.

STEP 9. DECIDE ON SCHEDULE

Top management must accept and willingly commit the time, staff, and resources required to do the planning. The size and complexity of the organization, with regard to services offered have some impact on the length of time needed to complete the cycle. Developing a strategic long-range plan for the MLC can take anywhere from 8 to 18 months. Keeping to 12 months or under is recommended, as a prolonged effort loses momentum and blankets enthusiasm. The amount of time will, of course, depend on the scale of the effort. Another consideration in deciding on the time frame is how much data is already available, how much must be collected, and the extent of the methods to be used. For example, MLCs that have long-range plans from member libraries and that consistently gather and report standard statistics may have some of the needs assessment completed. Others may have very few service statistics and few plans or evaluative reports to use. Such data gathering could take three to six months before the planning process can really get under way. Do keep in mind that no matter how much data is available, first-hand input from constituents will still need to be included and takes time to complete. Other factors that affect the time frame include the extent of previous interaction among and between the members of the planning team, and whether the planners have compatible views of the MLC's future. It takes time to develop a plan. Planning is a continuous process, its time frame is ongoing.

Once the overall time frame is estimated, use the process outline to schedule the major activity dates on a calendar and fill in with specifics and deadlines along the way. This provides a very

> *No matter how much data is available, first-hand input from constituents will still need to be included and takes time to complete.*

clear picture of the workload for the planning effort and immediately spots conflicts in time already committed or required for ongoing activities of the MLC. Now, the final time frame can be determined. Know that flexibility is a must and that time extensions are almost always to be planned for. *Example 6, Planning Process Time Line,* suggests a schedule for the planning process.

PRE-PROCESS Board okays planning; appoint plan coordinator

MONTH 1   Initiate data gathering
                 Begin planning to plan

MONTH 2   Appoint and charge Planning team, give them reading assignment
                 Hold KICK OFF meeting

MONTH 3   Planning team meets twice: identify data gaps and assign ESNA teams; train planning team
                 ESNA teams begin work
                 Send out first newsletter

MONTH 4   Vision and Mission meeting
                 ESNA teams working
                 Vision/Mission draft team prepares revised drafts

MONTH 5   Planning team meets twice: review Vision and Mission drafts, send out for input/comment and
                 develop planning outline; conduct Strengths, Weaknesses, Opportunities, Threats (SWOT)
                 exercise
                 ESNA Teams preparing reports
                 Send out second newsletter

MONTH 6   Planning Team meets twice: two ESNA teams report at each meeting; planning team lists key
                 concepts, issues etc. from reports

MONTH 7   Planning team meets once (plus retreat): two ESNA teams report, ideas/issues listed.
                 Hold planning retreat: cover synthesis of planning team's review of ESNA team reports; set
                 directions and some measures
                 Send out third newsletter

MONTH 8   Planning team meets twice: review retreat and affirm decisions, send out for comment; revisit
                 Vision and Mission statements

MONTH 9   Planning team members are represented at reaction meetings
                 Hold open meetings for reactions to the plan, i.e., goals, strategic directions, etc.
                 Plan coordinator and MLC director (and/or consultant) redraft plan

MONTH 10   Planning team meets twice: review input from reaction meetings and the redrafted plan; discuss
                 implementation and evaluation
                 Send out fourth newsletter

MONTHS 11   MLC board approval
                 Prepare plan for publishing

MONTH 12   Disseminate plan
                 Celebration

BEGIN IMPLEMENTATION!!!

only major activities are covered here, more marketing is essential and periodic board updates before approval, etc.

STEP 10. MARKETING THE PLANNING EFFORT

The tenth step is critical to the success of strategic planning. Its very easy to let it slide or say "we'll take care of that later." Marketing helps mobilize interest in the process, strengthens commitment to the MLC, and ensures support for planning activities and access to necessary resources. It is done BEFORE, DURING and AFTER the plan is developed. Use *Worksheet H, Marketing the Effort*, to develop a marketing plan for the MLC planning process.

Planning to Plan	Excerpt MARKETING THE EFFORT	Worksheet H
Activities Before During After	Who's Responsible	When, How Often

Before

Really "before" before, the MLC director must be sure the officers of the board are sold on planning so that they can sell it to the rest of the board.

Choose a way to kick off the process to share the purpose of the effort and set expectations for the plan. Hold an all-members meeting (or several if one is not practical) and have a futurist speaker or presentation on planning. Prepare a video message with wide distribution of the tapes.

Prepare the MLC staff, discuss the probable impact on the workload and prioritize major projects that could be effected by the planning process.

During

Decide on the target audience(s) for the plan. Is it primarily for government officials, for members, for the MLC board and staff, or for the end user, i.e., the members' publics? This will also help you decide on the plan format and distribution.

Strong participation in the process is the best marketing tool of all and will focus everyone on the shared set of goals. The use of task groups and already functioning committees has been mentioned earlier. These groups can do a great deal of the research and prepare reports for the planning committee while creating a sense of individual participation that cannot be gained any other way. A further benefit is that MLC and member staff are closer to the front line and have irreplaceable anecdotal information on services and end user needs.

Regularly communicate to all MLC staff and as many member staff as feasible. "Fertilize the grapevine," use the political system, incorporate planning updates in regular channels of communication, hold interviews with the directors of member libraries, and celebrate successes along the way.

27

Have selected people from the planning committee meet with staff and managers of member libraries during unit meetings. Use articles, reports, memos, and newsletters asking for reactions to new developments, seeking input and suggestions. Share assumptions, key environmental trends, clearly mandated needs. Then be sure to accept and act on recommendations that can be implemented and acknowledge the source. If it is not possible or appropriate, explain why.

Remember the larger community of members and non-members, their boards and trustees, government officials, key leaders in the area. Bring these people along so that when priorities are made they know why and so that, if they do not fit with some of their unique needs, it is not a shock or a cause for withdrawal.

After

Fit the message and the medium to the audience!

Distribute the published plan to the target audience. Write concise briefs or use executive summaries for members boards, staffs and politicians. Make personal presentations to member boards and the MLC board. Attend member staff meetings. Hold open meetings on the plan. Discuss implementation, monitoring and evaluating progress, the roles those involved are expected to play, and how the plan fits and impacts all members and their customers.

Prepare and distribute periodic updates on progress, successes, and problems.

In summary, the marketing goals regarding strategic planning are:
- Widespread participation
- Widespread understanding
- Helping others to be change agents
- Creating new possibilities
- An inclusive environment
- Implementing as a team

Purpose and Scope: _____

_____

_____

_____

_____

_____

_____

_____

Concerns/issues that must be addressed: _____

_____

_____

Time Frame for planning: Begin:_____ Disseminate plan: _____

Responsibilities:
WHO: director, whole board, board representatives, staff (names), governing body, consultants(s), community expert, state library agency consultant, others...

WHAT	ASSIGNED TO:
Plan coordination	_____
Data collection	_____
Meeting, decision making facilitation	_____
Vision, Mission meeting	_____
Planning team training	_____
Analyzing data gathered	_____
Plan writer	_____
Plan approval	_____
_____	_____
_____	_____

Planning Team Charge: _____

_____

_____

_____

_____

_____

_____

_____

_____

_____

_____

Planning Team Members: *use names and identify if representing a group*

Name	Phone	Assigned to call	Agreed to serve

Knowledge/skills needed:

* long-range planning
* writing plans
* facilitating meetings/decision making
* group and individual interviewing

*facilitating/training in visioning, etc.
*data collection and analysis
*survey development
*_____

Expertise Available:

MLC Staff:_____

_____

_____

_____

Board: _____

_____

Members:_____

_____

Outside
Assistance:_____

_____

Gaps in Expertise:_____

_____

_____

Hire Consultants to:_____

_____

PLANNING TO PLAN	OUTLINE AND SCHEDULE		WORKSHEET D

Use with the Marketing worksheet or incorporate marketing activities on this planning form.

Planning Activity	Who's Involved	Who Leads	Dates
Kick off:			
Planning Team education and training:			
Planning Team meetings:			
Develop Vision & Mission:			
ESNA and ESNA Teams:			
Develop strategic issues, goals, objectives/major strategies:			

PLANNING TO PLAN	OUTLINE AND SCHEDULE		WORKSHEET D cont.
Member review of draft goals and directions:			
Revisit Vision & Mission:			
Develop Actions and Implementation plans:			
Final draft plan review:			
Plan approval:			
Publish and disseminate plan:			
Celebration:			
Evaluate planning process:			

PLANNING TO PLAN	LEVEL OF EFFORT		WORKSHEET E

Based on the decisions about level of effort, fill in the basic, middle ground and extensive block.

Areas of Effort	Basic Level	Middle Ground	Extensive
WHO PLANS			
EXPERTISE NEEDED			
MARKETING the PLAN			
ENVIRONMENTAL SCAN NEEDS ASSESSMENT			
VISION, MISSION, VALUES			
SETTING DIRECTION			
IMPLEMENTATION			
MONITOR/ EVALUATE			

The first step in preparing a planning budget is to list all the major activities (refer to the completed Outline and Schedule worksheet) and then estimate the costs for all the elements that will make it happen.

Kick off

    announcement   photocopies: _____

                        postage: _____

    speaker fee and expenses: _____

    refreshments: _____

    other: _____

Planning team

    background materials/reports purchases: _____

    planning team notebooks: _____

    photocopies: _____

    travel: _____

    refreshments: _____

    meeting supplies (flip charts, paper, markers, etc.): _____

    other: _____

Marketing

    newsletter   photocopies: _____

                   postage: _____

    fliers/update sheets   photocopies: _____

                   postage: _____

    symbolic trinkets, thank-you gifts, etc.: _____

    other: _____

ESNA teams

    research materials/report purchases: _____

    teams   working photocopies: _____

                 reports photocopies: _____

    focus group refreshments: _____

    surveys   development: _____

                 postage: _____

    interviews   travel: _____

                 extra telephone: _____

    other: _____

Plan drafts and publication

    photocopies: _____

    layout: _____

    printing: _____

    postage: _____

    other: _____

<u>Vision, Mission meeting:</u>

    facilitator   fee: _____

                      expenses: _____

    conference room rental: _____

    photocopies: _____

    lunch: _____

    refreshments: _____

    supplies (flip charts, markers,

     overhead projector, etc):   _____

<u>Planning Retreat</u>

    facilitator   fee: _____

                      expenses: _____

    conference room rental: _____

    lodging: _____

    meals: _____

    travel: _____

    photocopies: _____

    supplies: _____

<u>Plan Review</u>

    facilitator   fee: _____

                      expenses: _____

    photocopies: _____

    refreshments: _____

    supplies: _____

<u>Planning Process Consultant</u>

    fee: _____

    expenses: _____

    telephone consultations: _____

<u>Celebration</u>

    handouts: _____

    wine & cheese: _____

    decorations: _____

Other: _____

_____

_____

_____

_____

_____

_____

PLANNING TO PLAN	PLANNING BUDGET	WORKSHEET G

This is the second step to preparing the planning budget. Add the costs for the like elements and put them in the MLC's familiar budgeting categories.

BUDGET CATEGORY	PROJECTED AMOUNT	SUBTOTALS
Staff/Committee Expenses		
conference room rental:	_____	
travel:	_____	
meals:	_____	
lodging:	_____	
refreshments:	_____	
other:	_____	_____
Meeting Supplies		
purchase of research materials:	_____	
notebooks:	_____	
flipcharts and paper:	_____	
markers, tape:	_____	
overhead, transparencies:	_____	
other:	_____	_____
Office Expenses		
photocopies:	_____	
postage:	_____	
extra telephone:	_____	
other:	_____	_____
Marketing Supplies		
decorations:	_____	
special paper:	_____	
gifts and trinkets:	_____	
other:	_____	_____
Publication Plan		
layout:	_____	
printing:	_____	
other:	_____	_____
Consultant/Facilitator/Speaker		
fee:	_____	
expenses:	_____	_____
		TOTAL_____

PLANNING TO PLAN   MARKETING THE EFFORT   WORKSHEET H

List the methods to be used to communicate the process and the plan to the targeted audiences -- be specific within each target, i.e., MLC board, MLC staff (managers, all staff), members (administrators, managers, staff), government officials (which ones), key stakeholders, and others. Include selected major activities listed here in the *Worksheet D, Planning Process, Outline and Schedule.*

Activities	**Who is Responsible**	**When, How Often**

BEFORE:

_____

_____

_____

_____

_____

_____

_____

DURING:

_____

_____

_____

_____

_____

_____

_____

_____

_____

_____

_____

_____

_____

AFTER:

_____

_____

_____

_____

_____

_____

WHAT IS IT?

The first part of ESNA, the environmental scan, is analyzing the local, state, and potentially, national environment in which the MLC must operate. It includes looking at demographics, societal and library trends, and governmental issues. The second part of ESNA, the needs assessment, is looking at the needs of current and potential MLC members and the needs of the MLC as an organization.

WHY DO IT?

Planning without an environmental scan and needs assessment (ESNA) is planning in a vacuum. The environmental scan helps the MLC to understand and respond to the local, state, and even national issues and trends that could impact local libraries. The needs assessment ensures that member and potentially non-member libraries' needs are met. Together, the environmental scan and the needs assessment allow the MLC to lead toward the future while meeting current needs. The ESNA can also demonstrate the MLC's commitment to planning to the library community and their stakeholders. Finally, the ESNA is the beginning point to identify strategic issues, goals, and strategic directions.

STEPS

1. Review ESNA methods and determine most relevant and feasible
2. Appoint ESNA teams to conduct environmental scan and needs assessment and to study relevant issues
3. Implement ESNA methods and prepare reports for the planning team

KEY IDEAS AND CONCEPTS

♦ MLCs need to conduct BOTH an environmental scan and a needs assessment
♦ Data collection can be narrowed but should include some open-ended methods as well
♦ ESNA teams can help in collecting the data
♦ Involve stakeholders as appropriate
♦ Multiple methods are available to conduct the ESNA

WORKSHEETS (at end of chapter)

Worksheet I	Decision Matrix for ESNA Methods	Worksheet K	Analysis of MLC Statistics
Worksheet J	Statistical Comparison of Member Libraries	Worksheet L	Line of Business Analysis
		Worksheet M	SWOT

PLANNING PROCESS

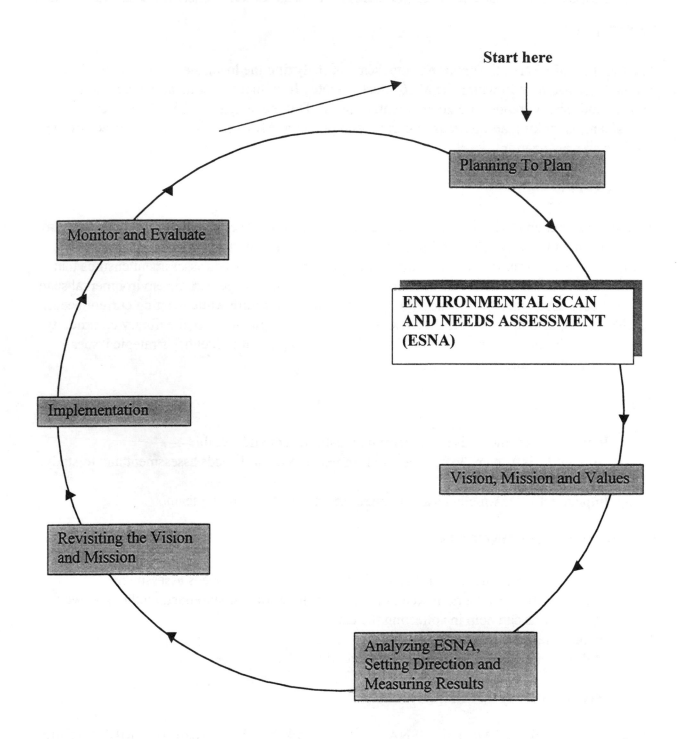

Start here

Planning To Plan

Monitor and Evaluate

ENVIRONMENTAL SCAN
AND NEEDS ASSESSMENT
(ESNA)

Implementation

Vision, Mission and Values

Revisiting the Vision
and Mission

Analyzing ESNA,
Setting Direction and
Measuring Results

PHASE II
ENVIRONMENTAL SCAN AND NEEDS ASSESSMENT (ESNA)

"Where all think alike, no one thinks very much."
Walter Lippman

INTRODUCTION

A key step in any planning effort is gathering information so that the planning team can make decisions about the MLC's program of services. An important point we have tried to make throughout this manual is that good planning depends on two factors: understanding what the people served say they need and looking into the future to see what they might need that they might not yet even be aware of.

An ESNA provides a realistic view of the current service programs and the local, state, and even national library and societal environment in which the MLC and its libraries must operate. It looks at needs of members and their communities. It can also help discern competitors whose service can impact the MLC.

The authors have coined a new term, ESNA, to remind MLC planners that both the environmental scan and a needs assessment must be done for the planning effort and resulting services to be most effective.

DEFINITIONS

There are two primary kinds of data gathering: environmental scan and needs assessment.

Environmental Scan is looking at the MLC from the outside. It is a look at the broader local, state, national, and even global environment in which the MLC must operate. It includes:
* members' stakeholders such as:
    - city/county leaders
    - school and academic boards
    - faculty and administrators
* demographics about users such as age, social characteristics, income, work, family size
    - economy and finances
    - political climate
    - geography factors
    - transportation
* state, national, and global trends
* government regulations
* trends in information technology and delivery
* competitors
* potential partners

All of these impact the MLC's development and operation and need to be examined.

<u>Needs Assessment</u> is looking at the MLC from the inside. It is a look at the MLC itself, the services it provides, and the needs of its members and potential members. It includes:
- member needs
- potential member needs
- needs of library users (as separate from demographics about them)
- MLC services and operation

The MLC functions as an entity itself with needs, problems, and a history of performance. Time should be taken to review how well the MLC has performed and what it needs as an organization in contrast to the needs of MLC members.

ESNA PROCESS

Deciding What Data to Collect

While an environmental scan and needs assessment is key to MLC planning, few MLCs have the resources, time, or will to gather all the potentially useful information available. This presents a dilemma. Determining what information to collect calls for a careful balance between being wide open to "what's out there" and circumscribing or selecting only a handful of topics or areas about which data is definitely needed.

The ESNA effort should include:
- research on topics already clearly known as critical issues
- open-ended research to identify hidden issues, needs, or trends that should not be overlooked

The information search can be narrowed in several ways:
- An important issue may have arisen as part of the scope or purpose of the planning process such as "the future of the MLC run community Free-Net" or "seeking new sources of income"

- A new statewide initiative may have arisen to which the MLC needs to respond (i.e., a new statewide electronic network, a state library initiative in continuing education, or new school standards)

- Current MLC services may need to be redesigned because of increasing or declining use (i.e., decrease in ILL or reference requests due to increased capability at the local level; increase in the need for courier or reciprocal borrowing because local library resources are on a statewide network)

- A quick review of existing data might uncover trends that the MLC should investigate (i.e., increasing number of senior citizens or an ethnic minority as determined by census figures).

The board, MLC director, and/or planning team may be able to identify these issues early and make sure that relevant information is collected that can be used in setting direction for the MLC. The selected areas/topics/issues will very likely be a basket of mixed fruit rather than a bowl of oranges. The tricky part is not becoming so narrowly and "now" focused that the effort is conducted with blinders on. Pre-select no more than a handful of issues/topics/issues so that there is room left for open-ended research. It is with open-ended research that the unknown challenges soon to impact the MLC, serendipitous new niches, and unarticulated member needs will emerge.

Who Collects the Data

In a smaller MLC, data/information collection might be done by the staff, providing relief is given from other job tasks. A highly inclusive way is to appoint ESNA teams. ESNA teams might include from 3-10 people made up of MLC staff, member library staff, community agency staff (depending on the issue), key stakeholders, even library school students. The more involvement in the planning process, the more buy-in for the plan. Some MLCs do business through member library staff committees. Using ESNA teams is a version of that practice, although it may be best to not use standing committees as the ESNA teams. This is an opportunity to get different people interacting with each other, to have more people involved, to ensure "new" thinking on old problems, and as much as possible to avoid vested interest in the outcome or recommendation.

> *This is an opportunity to get different people interacting with each other, to ensure "new" thinking on old problems, and, as much as possible, to avoid vested interest in the outcome or recommendation.*

The directing and coordinating of the ESNA effort is crucial. In *Phase I, Planning to Plan*, the data coordination responsibility is outlined. Whoever takes on the role--the plan coordinator, another staff person, or a consultant--will be the clearinghouse, the overseer, and the final synthesizer of the information for the planning team. All of the ESNA must be orchestrated so that each person/group's effort is synchronized and not duplicated, that findings and sources are shared across groups, and that the same people are not contacted by several of the groups for their input. Finally, the reports must be compiled in such a way that the planning team can develop goals and objectives.

Example 7, ESNA Team Organization and Effort, shows how the ESNA might be organized by an MLC. This shows an extensive level of effort choice with a data coordinator, six ESNA teams, the planning team, a consultant, and the MLC director involved.

- The data coordinator would be responsible for reviewing statistics, reports, and studies and long range plans besides acting as data coordinator.
- Team One is a large ESNA team comprised of a cross-section of members with expertise/interest is assigned the topic of technology--with specific focus on member library needs, MLC capabilities, and emerging trends.
- Team Two is selected for facilitation skills and objectivity (i.e., state library consultant staff or staff from another MLC) and is to conduct focus groups of key staff from member libraries to evaluate current MLC services and identify gaps and areas for improvement.
- Team Three is to conduct a continuing education survey of member and potential member staff that seeks current satisfaction and need and future topics and delivery methods for CE.
- Team Four works on cooperative collection development and document delivery with the charge to explore electronic alternatives.
- Team Five is to conduct a visioning exercise with representative directors from member libraries and key stakeholders (e.g., library school dean/faculty, library partners from the community, knowledgeable government officials, the state librarian) on library services in general and how libraries working together could better serve the people.
- Team Six, composed mostly of MLC staffers, is responsible for getting wide input and drafting the values statements.
- The consultant is to conduct a full SWOT with the planning team on member needs and environmental impacts, work with the data coordinator in synthesizing the data/team reports and facilitate the setting of direction and measuring the results phase.
- The MLC director (and/or members of the Board) interview representative government officials, community agency directors (current or potential library partners), the school superintendent and a few influential leaders regarding local needs and the opportunities for collaboration.

Two other possibilities are:
- Use the results of the member needs focus groups to develop a survey for wider member input
- Consider asking each library to conduct quick, random user surveys to gather data on specific services the MLC impacts, like interlibrary loan, or patron reserves, etc.

When using ESNA teams, be sure the teams are given clear charges and good directions. They will be checking-in with the data coordinator, getting approval before conducting any methods that contact members or stakeholders (surveys, focus groups, interviews), sharing information across groups, and combining efforts/questions when appropriate. Teams would start and end at different times but their task will have to be done with short turnaround as each ESNA team must report to the planning team that also has a tight schedule. The plan coordinator is overseer and ombudsman for the entire planning effort; therefore the data coordinator reports and works closely with the plan coordinator.

STRATEGIC ISSUES, MEMBER NEEDS AND TRENDS

It is suggested that three types of information be collected in the ESNA:

1. strategic issues
2. member needs
3. library and societal trends

Following is a brief definition and discussion of the three types of information and how they work together.

1. Strategic Issues

Issues that cross service or constituency lines. They are issues that are critical to the success of the organization. They can deal with funding, political realities, service problems, or any other issue that must be resolved before progress can be made in MLC operation or service. Some of these may be easily identified and assigned to an ESNA team early in the process.

John Bryson, in *Strategic Planning for Public and Non-profit Organizations* (page 104), defines a strategic issue as "fundamental policy questions or critical challenges that affect an organization's mandates, mission, and values, product or service level and mix; clients, users, or payers; or cost, financing, organization, or management."

Identifying strategic issues requires looking beyond individual services or specific member needs. It requires taking a broader view of the policy and/or operational issues that underlie an organization's program of service. If dealt with successfully, strategic issue resolution leads to more successful organizations. If ignored, strategic issues can hamper overall success, and particularly, growth.

2. Member Needs

Needs are an essential part of any planning process. Just what is it that members want from the MLC? Too often, members are avid with praise for MLC staff, appreciative of all services currently received, and not forthcoming with ideas for new services. Different data gathering techniques can be used to open up the conversation and get input from member libraries.

More information may be obtained from prospective member libraries about what services would entice them to join or take a greater part in MLC services. No planning process is complete that does not gather information from current or future members about the services they want and value.

3. Library and Societal Trends

A key role of MLC staff and board is leadership. This can be productively used when the MLC staff step back from day-to-day operations and look for trends that might impact the MLC service program. Such trends might include an increase or decrease in the overall use of a service; a statewide program that the MLC might participate in; an observation gained by looking at the statistical profile of member libraries.

The trick is to merge strategic issues, client needs, and trends into a coherent plan. Most planning guides focus on member needs or strategic issues and leave out trends all together. Leaving out one of these, however, seriously limits the resulting plan.

CHOOSING THE ESNA METHOD

Which methods are most relevant to the MLC's planning process depends on resources (dollars and people) available and time allotted. In choosing, care should be taken to ensure that both environmental scan AND needs assessment methods are specified. Doing only an environmental scan OR only a needs assessment leaves out an important set of data and information. ESNA teams assigned topics such as technology, cooperative collection development, or alternative funding mechanisms may choose from among these methods as appropriate. Whatever is chosen should be discussed and negotiated with the data coordinator.

It is most efficient to use the ESNA methods that look at existing data first before embarking on the ESNA methods that require the more extensive effort of contacting people. This can help the decision making process of choosing which more extensive ESNA methods might be used and what kinds of information might be best sought in focus groups, interviews, and surveys.

Worksheet I, Decision Matrix for ESNA Methods, helps planners and ESNA teams determine whether an ESNA method might be used with members, potential members, stakeholders or others.

ESNA		Excerpt DECISION MATRIX FOR ESNA METHODS			Worksheet I
Type of method	Used with members	Used with potential members	Used with stakeholders	Person/ ESNA team responsible to implement	Date to be completed

INVOLVING STAKEHOLDERS

Several of the ESNA methods described below suggest that stakeholders be involved in the collection of input and information. External stakeholders for an MLC include stakeholders of the member libraries. Gathering information from these members' stakeholders can help uncover what they want for the libraries they oversee and lead to a reconsideration of the kinds of services that an MLC can provide.

External stakeholders can include:

- Potential community partners
- Local governing officials
- State governing officials
- State librarian and staff
- School superintendents
- School principals
- School teachers

- Academic presidents/deans
- Academic professors
- Major corporations in the area
- Major foundations in the area
- Leaders of ethnic groups
- Leaders of demographic groups

ESNA METHODS

There are 10 ESNA methods/data sources described below.

1. Statistics, reports, and studies
2. Long-range plans
3. Strengths, Weaknesses, Opportunities, and Threats (SWOT)
4. Focus groups
5. Visioning
6. Interviews
7. Surveys
8. Group forums
9. Legal requirements and standards
10. Awareness and observation

Organization of this section:

Each of the ESNA methods is described separately and is presented in this manner:

METHOD

Introduction:

Requirements: What is necessary in terms of availability of data, staff effort, commitment of time for the MLC to use this method?

Level of Effort: Some of the methods described below can be done with information probably already available in the MLC office. Other methods require substantial preparation and expense to undertake and complete. As described in *Phase I, Planning to Plan, Step 7, Level of Effort*, progress from basic to extensive along a continuum.

Type of data: Whether the method is more likely to produce strategic issues, client needs, or trends.

Method Description: Instructions on how the method could be carried out.
How this Method Can Be Used in Needs Assessment:
How this Method Can Be Used in Environmental Scan:

After reading what is entailed in each of these methods, the planning team can use ESNA *Worksheet I, Decision Matrix for ESNA Methods,* to decide which methods will be used in the MLC planning effort.

ESNA METHOD 1
STATISTICS, REPORTS, AND STUDIES

In this method, statistics are gathered about the environment and the members, potential members, and the MLC.

Requirements:	Data on member libraries
	Data on potential member libraries
	Data on state or other area being compared
	Data about the MLC
	Person to analyze data and look for trends, strengths or weaknesses
Level of effort:	Minimal if statistics are available, extensive if they are not
Type of Data:	Strategic issues, client needs, trends

Method Description: There is much statistical gathering in the library community. Information about the statistical standing of libraries within the MLC is most likely available from the state library agency, however, not all state libraries collect all the information below and may not collect it for all types of libraries. Statistical information about the MLC can be gathered by the MLC. Often the state library also collects data from all MLCs within a state, or the MLC can seek comparative information from other MLCs directly. If the MLC does not currently collect data, now would be a good time to start. A survey can be designed to elicit the specific data needed.

Statistical information can be used in two ways. First, it can be used to compare the member or potential member libraries or MLC with themselves over time, or the data can be used to compare the member/non-member libraries or MLC with others in the state or across state lines.

How This Method Can Be Used in Needs Assessment--Statistics, Reports, and Studies
One place to start to determine member needs is to review available statistics about member libraries. Member statistics can be compared against other members in the region as well as against statewide performance statistics. ESNA *Worksheet J, Statistical Comparison of Member Libraries*, at the end of this chapter, indicates areas in which comparisons might be made and provides a way to compare one MLC to others of the same type.

ESNA *Worksheet J, Statistical Comparison of Member Libraries*, should be done for each type of library. (Excerpt below, full form at the end of the chapter) The data elements/area of service will change depending on the type of library being assessed.

ESNA	Excerpt STATISTICAL COMPARISON OF MEMBER LIBRARIES		Worksheet J
Type of Library Academic _____	Public _____	School _____	Special _____
Area of Service	Average of MLC		Average State/Multistate
Overall staffing			
Number of prof. Staff			

The ESNA Team should look for major differences, particularly weaknesses that might need to be addressed. Do the member libraries of the MLC have more or fewer Internet connections than other libraries around the state? Are the books of member libraries older or newer than comparative libraries? What is the staffing level of member libraries? For all of these: is there a reason and what should the MLC do about it?

If the MLC is interested in expanding membership, statistics about potential member libraries can also be examined. Are there similar characteristics about non-member libraries that might lead to their isolation from or non-participation in the MLC? Are needs identified that the MLC could meet with a new set of services?

The MLC should not overlook statistics about its own operation, compared to itself over time and to other MLCs in the state. Typical statistics that can be examined are shown in ESNA *Worksheet K, Analysis of MLC Statistics*, at the end of this section and an excerpt is shown here as an example. The items in the service column on the left will depend on the services offered by the MLC.

ESNA	Excerpt ANALYSIS OF MLC STATISTICS		Worksheet K	
Service	MLC		State/Multi-state	
	5 yrs ago	Now	5 yrs ago	Now
number of members				
average consulting visits per member				

Once the data is examined, the MLC can compare service use to itself over time or to other MLCs in the state. For example, is the member use of MLC ILL services increasing or decreasing? For all members or selective members? Is it time to wean members off of MLC ILL and train them to use a statewide database to go directly to the library that owns the book they want?

Finding these statistics, reports, and studies can be a challenge, but well worth the effort if it uncovers trends or opportunities that can benefit current or new MLC members.

Another way to look at the current MLC services is through a Line of Business (LOB) analysis. Each service offered by the MLC can be considered a line of business. Timothy Nolan in *Applied Strategic Planning in a Library Setting* described any given LOB as proceeding through four stages from emergence to decline:

Emergence: new LOB, low level of use, use building
Growth: use building rapidly
Maturity: rate of growth of use slows, use levels off, may be a slight decline
Decline: use reduces

For example, assistance with Web page construction may be in emergence phase but move into a growth phase within a year. Courier service may be in the maturity phase if all libraries are on a delivery route and stay at that level until electronic delivery escalates. Back-up reference service may be on the decline, as reference librarians become more self-sufficient.

The MLC can evaluate each of its services along this matrix using *Worksheet L, Lines of Business Analysis*. For each Line of Business, check the stage the service is in, using data to confirm the judgement.

ESNA	Excerpt LINES OF BUSINESS ANALYSIS			Worksheet L
Line of Business	Emergence	Growth	Maturity	Decline

How This Method Can Be Used in Environmental Scan--Statistics, Reports, and Studies
Statistics can also be used to determine general trends or strategic issues about the state or region. Is the economy expanding or contracting? Does this produce more or less resources for the MLC or member libraries to contribute to MLC programs or services? Is the population (or parts of it) increasing or decreasing? Is there an influx of senior citizens, younger families with pre-schoolers, ethnic minorities, or immigrants? Does this lead the MLC toward a program to help member libraries serve this growing population? Are there new needs of local businesses that MLCs could assist member libraries to serve, perhaps in the area of automation?

The planning team might also examine studies and reports from the state or region. If the State Department of Education adopted standards-based education, what could the MLC do to assist school media centers to participate in this effort in their local school districts? If the state library established new standards for public, school, or academic libraries, what can the MLC do to help local libraries meet the new standards? If there was a new state or regional effort to connect communities, schools, hospitals, or businesses electronically, what can the MLC do to help local libraries participate in this effort? If there was a new grant opportunity that libraries can benefit from, what can the MLC do to help its members get part of this money?

ESNA METHOD 2
LONG-RANGE PLANS

Long range plans of members and potential members can be a valuable source of information.

Requirements: Members and potential members have long-range plans
                    available to the MLC
                    Person to analyze long-range plans
Level of effort: Moderate if the information is available
                    Intensive if MLC staff must assist local libraries in developing long-range
                    plans or if there are many members
Type of data: Strategic issues, client needs, trends

Method Description: One source of information that an MLC can use to plan its services is the long-range plans of its members, non-members, and local communities. Presumably, these long-range plans will indicate the needs and directions in which the local libraries or communities wish to go. By looking for commonalities among these long-range plans, the MLC can frequently discover areas in which MLC members need assistance. This information can be used to discover collective needs that might be the focus of long-range goals or objectives or simply provide ways to provide consulting or technical assistance to individual libraries. The MLC should review its own long-range plan and look at those of other MLCs in the state or region.

How This Method is Used in Needs Assessment--Long-Range Plans
Review plans of members and potential members as described above looking for similarities about which the MLC can focus services. Similarities in the need statements, goals, objectives, and/or activities within these plans can guide the MLC. Look for similarities among the same type or size of library and between different types and sizes of libraries. This may be a source of particularly useful ideas to meet member needs.

As part of this process, the MLC should look at its own long-range plan and those of other MLCs in the state (or nationally, if a multistate MLC). If the MLC already has a long-range plan, have the goals and objectives been met? To what extent? If the planning team can't tell, it may indicate a need to be more specific and do a better job of measuring performance in the future. Copies of the long-range plans from other MLCs might provide some insight into trends or programs that the MLC could consider.

How This Method is Used in Environmental Scan--Long Range Plans
It is also possible to go the extra step and review the long-range plans of the members' parent institutions such as the colleges or universities within the MLC, the school districts, or the local government entities. These might unearth trends that cross institutional lines and impact the development or even existence of the library. Alternatively, specific elements of each community's development could be surveyed, keyed to MLC needs.

For example, do local school district plans refer to how and of what quality school library media services will be delivered? Can the MLC intervene to advocate for better school library media services? Can the MLC offer to supervise media services (for a price)?

ESNA METHOD 3
STRENGTHS, WEAKNESSES, OPPORTUNITIES AND THREATS
(SWOT)

The *SWOT* is a method that identifies current strengths and weaknesses, and future opportunities and threats that face the MLC. It is a particularly good tool for both an environmental scan and a needs assessment.

Requirements:	Someone who understands the process and can facilitate the discussion
	About three hours of time
	Can be done with any size group but a larger group will take a longer time
Level of effort:	Moderate, in that it requires bringing people together who are willing to commit the time. When a consultant is used, there is additional expense.
Type of data:	This is an excellent tool for identifying strategic issues and trends.

Method Description: The *SWOT* exercise can be used in two places in the planning effort. It is a traditional technique often used to begin discussions in a planning effort and with focus groups or community forums to gather initial input. It can also be used to help guide the data collection process. Used in *Phase IV, Analyzing Data and Setting Direction*, it can be used to help select the important aspects of all data being collected.

ESNA	Excerpt	Worksheet N
	INSTRUCTIONS FOR CONDUCTING A FULL SWOT	

1. STRENGTHS +	4. OPPORTUNITIES +
INTERNAL	INTERNAL
EXTERNAL	EXTERNAL
2. WEAKNESSES -	3. THREATS -
INTERNAL	INTERNAL
EXTERNAL	EXTERNAL

In this exercise, participants are divided into small groups and then brainstorm events, happenings, or issues that fall into each quadrant. Participants have the opportunity to look at both internal and external factors in all quadrants as well as to focus on the strengths and weaknesses in the present and the threats and opportunities to be faced in the future.

After the brainstorming is completed, participants choose the most critical issues in each quadrant. This can be done based on perceived importance, criticality of the issue, or appearance in more than one quadrant. In fact, it is not unusual for the same issue to appear in more than one quadrant. For example, technological capacity may be a strength in large libraries, a weakness in small libraries, a threat to some librarians, and a tremendous opportunity to better serve the public.

After all small groups have chosen their top issues, each small group shares with the large group and together they discuss all issues, combine similar issues, and eventually vote as a large group on the most critical issues that the MLC is addressing. This is an excellent way to identify strategic issues, goals, and strategic directions. The items listed in three or four quadrants typically get at larger systemic issues.

Many planning efforts stop after the brainstorming part of a *SWOT*. The final step in this process is for the planning team to look at each strategic issue and brainstorm what, if any, response is appropriate from the MLC. These issues and responses can become part of the written plan and their integration into the full plan is discussed in *Phase IV, Analyzing ESNA.*

How This Method Can Be Used In Needs Assessment--SWOT

SWOT is an excellent tool to use with members and potential members, who can provide valuable and knowledgeable input about the MLC and the climate in which they operate. The *SWOT* can be done by the planning team, small groups in a membership meeting, or subgroups of member staff (children's librarians, catalogers). Comparing the various results among groups can lead to valuable insights.

The *SWOT* can be used with the MLC board or MLC staff (assuming there are enough of them!). As the external focus may be more useful with stakeholders, the internal focus may be more useful with the MLC board and staff.

How this Method Can Be Used in Environmental Scan--SWOT

The *SWOT* can be done with stakeholders, boards, and administrators of member libraries. The results may not be as useful on internal issues and services because the participants may not be as knowledgeable. The information gained about **external** strengths, weaknesses, opportunities, and threats may be more relevant to the planning effort. This group is more likely to identify environmental trends that impact the MLC rather than to have information about the MLC services themselves.

If the external focus is emphasized, it may be useful to actually ask for strengths, weaknesses, opportunities, and threats in specific external categories such as:

- economic
- political/governmental
- social
- environmental
- geographic (rural/urban)
- technological
- human resources

ESNA METHOD 4
FOCUS GROUPS

Focus groups allow input to be gathered from small groups and for the MLC to ask questions the MLC specifically wants addressed:

Requirements:	Someone to develop and test the questions
	Someone objective to lead the focus groups
	Someone to record comments of participants
	People willing to participate in the focus groups
Level of effort:	Moderate to advanced
	Requires time to develop questions, organize, and conduct the focus groups and then to transcribe and analyze the results. Could include the cost of a moderator for the focus groups unless someone can be found

locally to do this. Unstructured focus groups (see below) require a more skilled facilitator than a structured focus group.

Type of data: Client needs, strategic issues

Method Description: Focus groups have become very popular as a way for groups to obtain information about a library or an MLC's service program. Typically, a focus group would have between 7 -15 people depending on the format chosen and last about 2 hours.   Groups smaller than 7 may not produce enough information and groups larger than 15 may prevent some people from participating.

A requirement of a focus group is that it be facilitated by someone who is perceived to be objective and DOES NOT participate in the discussion's content. There must be someone recording the comments made by participants on flip chart paper so that participants can see what is being recorded.

There are two kinds of focus groups: structured and unstructured. In the structured focus group, specific questions are asked and the answers are typically not probed in much depth. A great deal of ground can be covered in this approach.   Specific questions are asked in a specific sequence and the answers are recorded on flip chart paper.

At the conclusion of questions, the focus group facilitator can assist group members to merge like statements or eliminate duplicates in preparation for prioritizing among the statements made. Group participants can be asked to "vote" on the current services, changes, new services, issues, or trends that they believe are most important for the MLC to address in its strategic plan. Typically, participants are allowed a set number of votes (N/3 = number of items on flip chart paper divided by 3) and their votes are cast with magic marker pens or sticky dots. The results of the prioritization are tabulated, discussed with the focus group members, and conveyed to the planning team.

Unless politically necessary, these authors recommend that MLC staff NOT be participants in focus groups for members or potential members. Participants may feel they cannot criticize any MLC programs if staff are present and staff may feel the need to either explain and educate or be defensive. If it is necessary that staff be present, they should NOT be the facilitator and they should NOT participate in any way. Results may not be valid if staff are present.

In an unstructured focus group situation, the facilitator poses questions and depending on the answers, probes reasons for the answer. For example, if the question is asked: "What MLC services are most important to you," the facilitator would follow up the answers with questions like: why is it important? what role does it play in your library's service? what would you do if this service were not available? how might the service be changed to better serve you?

There are trade-offs in using the structured vs. the unstructured formats.

Structured Focus Groups	Un-Structured Focus Groups
Can handle 10 - 15 people.	Groups need to be smaller, between 7-10 people.
Can accommodate more questions of the group but discussion is not in-depth. Use when there are a broad range of questions to be asked.	Fewer questions can be asked but discussion is more in-depth. Use when there are two or three very specific issues to be discussed.
Discussion is structured, controlled by the facilitator.	Discussion is led by facilitator, but is more freewheeling because it goes in the direction dictated by participants.
Discussion is typically recorded on flip charts.	Discussion is typically recorded on tape or with a dedicated note taker.
Items listed can be easily prioritized.	Prioritization is difficult.

Whichever method is chosen, focus groups are a popular method of gathering information.

How This Method is Used in Needs Assessment--Focus Groups
This is an excellent tool to use with member libraries' representatives, with potential members, and with the planning team. The following kinds of questions (but not all of them) could be asked in a structured or unstructured format. Questions should be carefully framed so they are clear and not leading. Only 3 or 4 major questions should be asked overall.
- What MLC services are most valuable to you?
- What changes would you like to see in MLC services?
- What new services would you like to see delivered by the MLC?
- What major issues is the MLC facing?
- What major trends do you see that would impact MLC services?
- What is your opinion of (need for) _____ (a specific service that might be under consideration for initiation or elimination?)

The following questions might be asked with potential members:
- For what reason have you chosen not to join the MLC?
- What services that the MLC does not offer might be most useful to you?
- What might help you join the MLC?

Staff can be asked to participate in a focus group similar to the one used with clients but focusing primarily on the MLC itself.

How This Method Can Be Used in Environmental Scan--Focus Groups
The following kinds of questions might be asked with stakeholders:
- What issues are your library facing now and in the future?
- What are the greatest needs of the libraries with which you work?
- What kinds of assistance do these libraries need from outside the organization?

ESNA METHOD 5
VISIONING

Visioning allows library staff and library stakeholders to think "out of the box" about the preferred future of the library. It can be used to identify ways to reach that future.

Requirements:	Someone to lead the visioning exercise
	A group willing to participate in the process
Level of Effort:	Moderate
Types of Data:	Typically, needs of member libraries and their users

Method Description: A detailed discussion of creating a vision for the MLC is in Phase III. Here the focus is on how a visioning exercise can be used with multiple groups. As with the *SWOT*, the visioning exercise is usually used as a way to stimulate thinking. Whether used as a thinking stimulator or a more in-depth planning tool, the visioning exercise can be used with multiple groups.

How This Method Can Be Used in Needs Assessment--Visioning
Visioning is a good method to use in kicking off the planning process with key MLC stakeholders such as the planning team, the board, or staff. This is a method where staff, members, and board can participate together. It can be used with a large group, such as a full membership council, if the participants are broken into small groups. It can also be used with potential members to gather input about what kind of an MLC would best serve them.

How This Method Can Be Used in Environmental Scan-- Visioning
Visioning can also be used with non-librarians, but they are less likely to have a clear vision of what the MLC does now and may not be able to relate it successfully to the future. Used with non-librarians the exercise would have them think about library service in general; how all types of libraries working together might benefit their clientele or the public at large.

ESNA METHOD 6
INTERVIEWS

Interviews are a way to provide personal attention to key people and get in-depth and considered input from them. They can be used with key board members, member librarians, or non-library stakeholders.

Requirements:	Someone objective to do the interviews and report the results
	People willing to be interviewed
Level of Effort:	Advanced
	Time is required to construct, conduct, and report the interviews and cost could include a consultant unless someone on the planning team has the time to devote to the interviews. Can be very time consuming depending on the number of people chosen to be interviewed.

Types of data: Can include strategic issues, client needs, and trends depending on the questions that are asked.

Method Description: Personal interviews with single individuals or very small groups of two or three people allow for discussion that is concentrated and focused. The value of the personal interview is that it honors the person(s) being interviewed by focusing attention on them and their opinions. Because it is one-on-one (or one-on-a-few) it encourages interviewees to think about what they want to say and speak more thoughtfully.

It is also helpful to provide a list of questions in advance to interviewees so they can think about the answers and possibly gather information from others. Some interviewees even prepare written notes or responses (although that is not usually required). Confidentiality of an individual respondent's comments should be guaranteed, although the content may be used without attribution.

Questions to be asked could include the same as asked in the structured focus group, but with considerably more probing about the responses received. If there is a particular issue or problem that needs to be addressed, it can be included in the questions asked. Once all the interviews are completed, the results need to be analyzed to identify commonalities among the interviewees and to determine whether any strategic issues are raised that need to be dealt with.

The results of the interviews are integrated into all the other data gathered to be included in the decisions made about final goals and strategic objectives.

How This Method Can Be Used in Needs Assessment--Interviews
Possible people who could be interviewed as part of the needs assessment include:
* key library or school media directors or staff members
* MLC Board members
* MLC staff
* MLC potential members

Questions that could be asked include:
* MLC strengths and weaknesses
* key trends
* strategic issues facing the MLC
* problems that must be dealt with
* greatest success of the MLC in the past two years
* area where greatest improvement is needed
* one main new direction the MLC should take

How This Method Could Be Used in Environmental Scan--Interviews
Interviews can be held with people outside of the immediate MLC environment. For example:

- stakeholders for member libraries (elected officials, school boards)
- a major legislator
- futurists
- the state librarian
- other MLC directors
- community agency partners
- library school dean/faculty

The questions would differ depending on the person being interviewed, but might cover state or regional trends or local library needs that the MLC might serve.

ESNA METHOD 7
SURVEYS

Surveys are a useful method to gather information from a large group of like people. They require careful thought about the questions to be asked and to whom the survey should be administered. However, more information can be gathered from surveys than from almost any other method.

Requirements: Someone to develop the survey
     Someone to distribute the survey
     Someone to tabulate and analyze the survey

Level of effort: Advanced because of the cost to develop, distribute, tabulate and analyze the survey. Survey development and administration usually requires more expertise than other forms of data gathering.

Types of data: Best used to gather client needs

Method Description: Surveys are frequently used by MLCs to elicit from members (and potential members) their opinions about the MLC service program. A review of the plans submitted for the *Samples and Examples* manual revealed several types of information that is requested through surveys. Information is often collected by type of library so that any differences in opinion or needs from different types of libraries can be responded to by the MLC.

- what services are most used
- how services are ranked in terms of importance
- how well services are delivered
- benefits to the library from services provided
- opinion about new services that might be initiated
- some demographic information
- continuing education needs often arranged by possible topic
- library needs
- ability to serve on MLC committees
- what needs are met by entities other than the MLC
- information that would help governing bodies better deal with library issues

- technology needs for hardware, software, connectivity, training
- strengths and weaknesses

Most questions are multiple choice with few open ended questions so that the survey can be answered relatively quickly and more easily tabulated. Care should be taken to resist the temptation to include lots of questions because "it would be interesting to know that." It is usually helpful to get professional advice in designing a survey to make sure the questions are worded so that they are clear, non-contradictory, and can be tabulated in the easiest way possible. All surveys should be pre-tested before full distribution.

Once returned, the results can be analyzed for each question and possible use of demographic information used to see whether type or size of library makes a difference in the respondents' opinions or needs. Many surveys of MLC clients confirm that the MLC is already doing an excellent job of serving its members and, in fact, may suggest that no or few changes need to be made. This is why it is imperative that additional means of collecting information about the environment and less direct means of collecting information about client need be used.

How This Method Can Be Used in Needs Assessment--Survey
This method is best used with members or potential members or specific subgroups.

How This Method Can Be Used in Environmental Scan--Survey
The survey method can also be used with specific stakeholder groups such as:
- all school superintendents or school boards of member school libraries
- all city council/county council officials of member libraries
- all state legislators serving the area
- businesses serving the area

Questions asked on these surveys would deal more with the environment in which the local library operates and what these people see as:
- local library needs and performance
- strategic issues
- economic, social, and demographic trends that impact the library, community, or state

ESNA METHOD 8
GROUP FORUMS

Group forums are large meetings at which the long-range plan is discussed. It is often the membership group of the MLC. If used as part of the initial data gathering, the method is often combined with visioning or a *SWOT*. It can also be used to review a draft of the plan and that purpose is discussed below.

Requirements:	Facilitator who is not defensive about the plan
	Recorder to record on flip-chart paper or transparencies
Level of Effort:	Moderate. Inexpensive unless a consultant must be hired

Type of Data: Client needs

Method Description: Forums are large group meetings with 20 or more people. It is very difficult to work with this large a group using the questions or format of a focus group. Too many people tend to remain quiet, and difficult issues are rarely brought up unless they have already reached the crisis stage. However, sometimes the reality of the planning process dictates that large group forums be held.

How This Method Can Be Used in Needs Assessment--Group Forums

Member forums can be used in two ways. First, during the planning process, it may be necessary to explain the planning process and obtain input from the members in a large group session. While the depth of discussion may not equal that of a focus group, the forum should not replace focus groups--useful information can still be gathered. The membership forum can be used as the location of the first part of the *SWOT* exercise, focusing on the brainstorming. By dividing members into smaller groups, people can be encouraged to talk.

Membership meeting forums are often best used in reviewing an early draft of a plan. The planning team can present the results of its needs assessment and environmental scan. Indicate which direction the planning team is considering through goals/strategic directions, and share what measures of success are being planned. It allows the planning team to gather feedback about the proposed plan and to seek ideas about what success would look like to members. Participants can also be asked for suggestions to implement the strategic directions. The draft plan can be distributed in advance and covered step-by-step, giving participants an opportunity to comment on each aspect of the plan.

How This Method Can Be Used in Environmental Scan--Group Forums

Group forums have also been successfully used with non-library groups. In this situation questions should focus on the local library:

- what does your library do best?
- what can your library do to improve service?
- what help might your library need?

The results of these questions can lead to needed services that the MLC can provide.

ESNA METHOD 9
LEGAL REQUIREMENTS AND STANDARDS

Every MLC has legal requirements that it must adhere to, whether the requirements come from the state or the organization's bylaws.

Requirements: Someone to look at law, rules, or charter
Level of effort: Basic
Type of data: Could be trend or strategic issue or neither

Method Description: All MLC planning efforts should include a review of the law that governs the MLC. Often, as MLCs grow and evolve, the MLC operation varies from the law. Sometimes this review results in efforts to change or expand or clarify the law or charter that established the MLC or governs its operation. Care should be taken that no new service or activity violate the MLC's 501-C3 status.

For example, the Colorado law that governs MLCs specifically grants all powers of public library boards of trustees to the MLC Board except the ability to purchase property. Any goal of a Colorado MLC that involves the purchase of property would have to be abandoned or the law would have to be changed.

Several states have laws that specify that MLCs provide technical assistance, continuing education, and resource sharing. Some reference to these services needs to be included in any plan.

Hopefully, this review will be routine and the resulting plan will easily meet all legal requirements. However, the review could result in major efforts to revise some aspect of the legal foundation of the MLC and involve working with other MLCs in the state or the state library to change the law or rules.

There may also be standards for MLCs or standards for member libraries. The Association of Specialized and Cooperative Library Agencies published *Standards of Cooperative and Multitype Library Organizations* in 1990. These standards describe basic principles of how MLCs should be organized, governed, and operated. MLCs considering these basic elements may wish to refer to these standards for guidance.

Many states also have standards for academic, public, and school libraries. A major role of many MLC's is to help member libraries achieve these standards.

ESNA METHOD 10
AWARENESS AND OBSERVATION

Requirements: Someone with a keen observing eye

Level of Effort: Should be basic, but could be moderate if efforts are made to seek trends from various sources

Type of data: Strategic issues

Method Description: Every MLC and its members are impacted by state and regional trends. Many of these trends will surface if the *SWOT* is used. This method, however, can focus directly on trends and seek to articulate them. This can best be done by the MLC director or planning team member asking: How can I find out the major trends impacting libraries? The answers can be found in various sources:

- literature scan: major trends is a popular topic in the library press

61

- interviews: the state librarian, a major legislator, futurists all will have an opinion about major trends facing local libraries or the MLC
- attendance at national conferences

Much information is available to an MLC director or staff, almost through osmosis. It is information observed through participation in state wide committees, conversations with library leaders and other MLC directors across the state, from legislative relationships, through attendance at state and national library conferences. The ASCLA Interlibrary Cooperation and Networking Section meets regulary at each conference and has discussion groups that allow MLC staff to share concerns and successes. All of these provide information to the MLC director or staff that can be used to stimulate thinking and to identify strategic issues for the planning team. It is the role of catalyst, advocate, and leader in a data gathering mode.

ESNA is the foundation of planning. Through the needs assessment we get our answers to the key planning questions of: Who are our customers? Where are we now? With the environmental scan, we begin to address: where are we going?

ESNA	DECISION MATRIX FOR ESNA METHODS				WORKSHEET I
Type of method	Used with members	Used with potential members	Used with stakeholders	Person/ESNA team responsible	Date to be completed
Statistics, reports and studies					
Long-range plans					
SWOT					
Focus groups					
Visioning exercise					
Interviews					
Surveys					
Forums					
Legal requirements and standards					
Awareness and observation					
Other					

ESNA	LINES OF BUSINESS ANALYSIS			WORKSHEET L
Line of Business	Emergence	Growth	Maturity	Decline

Purpose of the SWOT
- Develop a list of issues of importance to the MLC
- Enable participants to achieve a clear and common understanding of factors that effect the MLC:
  - positive and negative
  - current and future
  - internal and external

Resources
Time: 2.5 to 3.5 hours for Steps 1-8
Equipment: Overhead projector OR flip chart stand
Supplies: Flip chart paper
             Magic markers
             Masking tape
             Pre-made transparencies or flip charts on the SWOT definition, chart, and criteria for importance
             Copies of *Worksheet M, SWOT* and definitions of Criteria for Importance for all participants

Suggested Procedure
Step 1:   (5 minutes) Welcome and thank participants, make appropriate introductions, and state the objectives of the procedure.

Step 2:   (10 minutes) Using a transparency or flip chart. The facilitator describes, step by step, what the SWOT chart will look like. *Worksheet M* is distributed at the end of the presentation. When the small groups actually discuss strengths, weaknesses, opportunities, or threats, they can record their discussion on large flip chart sheets.

        A.   Draw a vertical line dividing the page and then a horizontal line dissecting the vertical line

B.   In Box 1, write the word STRENGTH, put a plus (+) next to it to remind people it is a positive. Write the word *current* to remind us a strength is something that presently exists.

STRENGTH + (current)	

C.   In Box 2, write the word OPPORTUNITY, put a plus next to it to remind people it is positive, and write the word *future* to remind people an opportunity is something good that can "reasonably be anticipated in the foreseeable future."

STRENGTH + (current)	OPPORTUNITY + (future)

D.   Draw a dotted horizontal line dividing the two top boxes in half. In the top half, write the Word *Internal*. In the bottom half, write the word *External*. Internal refers to something about the organization itself. External refers to something about the larger world in which the organization operates.

STRENGTH + (current) Internal ------------------------ External	OPPORTUNITY + (future) Internal ------------------------ External

E.   Repeat steps 3 to 5 for WEAKNESS and THREAT with the same explanation, except that these are negatives.

STRENGTH + (current) Internal -------------------------- External	OPPORTUNITY + (future) Internal ------------------------- External
WEAKNESS - (current) Internal -------------------------- External	THREAT - (future) Internal ------------------------- External

Step 3:   (5 minutes) Use a transparency or flip chart to explain to the group that "opportunities" and "threats" relate to <u>trends</u> that may impact the organization, not actions the organization might take to respond to a trend. The trend areas are:

Demographic	Social	Economic
Governmental	Human Resources	Natural Resources
Technological	Scientific	Other

Step 4:   (5 minutes) Divide the large group into small groups of 4-10 people. Ask each small group to suggest a scribe to record the group's discussion and decision.

Step 5:   (20 minutes) Assign each group two boxes to complete giving each group either strengths and threats OR weaknesses and opportunities. This allows every group to discuss both positive and negative and present and future.   (It is possible to have all groups complete all four quadrants, but this doubles the time needed to complete this part of the process.)   Explain the two rules of the procedure:

Rule 1:   Be inclusive. Using the collective wisdom and experience of the small group, write as many factors in each box assigned (both internal and external) as possible. It is permissible to ask other group members what they mean by a factor. It is <u>not</u> permissible to offer an opinion or judgement about the value or rightness of the idea.

Rule 2:   Each individual participant has the responsibility to ensure that all other participants in the small group are actively contributing to the discussion.

Initiate small group discussions by reminding the scribes to keep a record and telling the groups they will have 15 to 20 minutes for their deliberations.

Step 6: (5-10 minutes) Ask the scribes to record their small group's findings on flip chart paper. Have the participants take a 5-10 minute break while the scribes complete this task. Have the scribes post the newsprint on a wall using masking tape. (To save time, ideas can be recorded directly on flip chart paper by the scribe but it produces a messier presentation).

Step 7: (20 minutes) After the break, explain to the small groups that all the factors they listed are important. To focus limited resources, however, it is necessary to identify which factors are most important. Using a previously prepared transparency or flip chart, explain the three criteria for importance. Ask each small group to use the three criteria to identify 20% of the factors listed in each box they were assigned that are the most important. These factors will be called "critical areas." The scribe can circle the identified "critical areas" on the flip chart paper.

Criteria for Importance:

Impact: A measure of "breadth" of importance. How basic is the factor? How many other things depend on it or are related to it?

Consequence: A measure of "depth" of importance. How bad or good will it be if we:
- *(a)   maintain the strength*
- *(b)   take advantage of the opportunity*
- *(c)   fail to correct the weakness*
- *(d)   adequately address the threat*

Immediacy: A measure of the importance of time. How much time is available:
- *(a)   before the strength will be lost if it is not nurtured*
- *(b)   to correct the weakness before it causes severe damage*
- *(c)   to take advantage of the opportunity before it disappears*
- *(d)   to prepare for the threat before it is too late to successfully address it*

Step 8: (30 minutes) Each sub-group should share with the entire group the list of all items mentioned and the 20% identified as critical issues. Allow for questions and answers about what is meant by any statement. Discussion about the merit or value of any statement is inappropriate at this time. (If the group is large, sub-groups might be asked to report only the "critical areas" they identified.) Note any overlaps that occur among three or four quadrants. These are candidates to be "strategic issues" or "strategic directions" or "goals" in the planning process and need to be addressed in some way by the organization.

If no further steps will be taken at this time, remind the participants that their statements will go to the planning team.

Steps 9 -13 represent a continuation of the procedure, working either with the original group or with the planning team.

Step	With original SWOT group	With planning team
Step 9	(5 minutes) If continuing with the same group, after a 10-15 minute break, ask the groups to reform with new people in each group.	Use this part of the process with the planning team.
Step 10	(20-30 minutes) Assign each sub-group two sets of critical areas to address. Assign strengths and threats or weaknesses and opportunities. Distinctions between internal and external are no longer relevant at this point. Ask each group to determine what the "response" of the organization should be to the critical area. (If the same critical area is in more than one quadrant, it should be dealt with by each of the sub-groups assigned a relevant quadrant.) A "response" could be an action, a new program, a change in how things are done, etc. Each group should select a scribe to record the group's decision. (Previous scribes can be exempted!)	Same process is done. If the planning team is large, divide into two groups. If the planning team is small, the entire group can discuss the critical areas in all four quadrants. This allows the group to better deal with overlapping critical areas.
Step 11	(5 minutes) Ask the scribes to record the small group's recommendations on flip chart paper and post on the wall.	Same. Post on wall so all can see the results of the group's work.
Step 12	(10 minutes) Have each small group report its recommendations. If the group is large, the facilitator can review a sample of the recommendations. Judgements about the merit or value of an idea are not appropriate at this point in the planning process.	If the planning team has been divided into small groups, each group should report. Judgements about the merit or value of an idea should be suspended at this point in the process.

Step 13	(5 minutes) Indicate that the results of the discussion will be passed on to the planning team or organization board. Review what the participants have accomplished and celebrate their efforts.	(5 to 60 minutes) Once all ideas are listed the planning committee or board can adjourn the discussion. Alternatively, the planning team can merge the results of the SWOT with other information gathered and begin to develop strategic issues, goals/strategic directions and objectives/measures of success.

The SWOT can be used to generate many ideas from a broad range of people. Carried to its full implementation, it can also produce MLC response for the planning team to consider. Done by the planning team as part of the setting direction process, it can be the centerpiece of determining strategic issues, goals/strategic directions and objectives/measures of success.

CRITERIA FOR IMPORTANCE DEFINITIONS

Impact: A measure of "breadth" of importance. How basic is the factor? How many other things depend on it or are related to it?

Consequence: A measure of "depth" of importance. How bad or good will it be if we:
- (a) maintain the strength;
- (b) take advantage of the opportunity;
- (c) fail to correct the weakness;
- (d) adequately address the threat?

Immediacy: A measure of the importance of time. How much time is available:
- (a) before the strength will be lost if it is not nurtured;
- (b) to correct the weakness before it causes severe damage;
- (c) to take advantage of the opportunity before it disappears;
- (d) to prepare for the threat before it's too late to successfully address it?

ESNA	SWOT STRENGTHS, WEAKNESSES, OPPORTUNITIES, THREATS,	WORKSHEET M

STRENGTHS (+) Present

INTERNAL

- -

EXTERNAL

OPPORTUNITIES (+) Future

```
TRENDS

DEMOGRAPHIC
SOCIAL
ECONOMIC
GOVERNMENTAL
HUMAN RESOURCES
NATURAL RESOURCES
TECHNOLOGICAL
SCIENTIFIC
OTHER
```

WEAKNESSES (-) Present

INTERNAL

- -

EXTERNAL

THREATS (-) Future

- -

WHAT IS IT?

Vision is the MLC's preferred future that, like a lighthouse, leads the way to success. Mission is the MLC's purpose, describing the business of the organization. Values are the code of behavior the MLC aspires to.

WHY DO IT?

In one brief page, all the individuals, groups, and organizations that interact with or are affected by the organization know why the MLC exists, what it does, and how it wishes to conduct its business. With a publicly stated vision, mission, and values, the MLC has an accepted guide for establishing partners and making decisions.

STEPS
1.   Create a Vision
2.   Draft or revise a Mission statement
3.   Articulate the values
4.   Keep statements as drafts until the goals and major strategies are identified

KEY IDEAS & CONCEPTS

♦   Vision is a future state
♦   Seek broad input and selected reaction
♦   Mission is what is now and describes the MLC's market niche
♦   Clarify values or principles, beliefs, philosophy   forget the differences in terms
♦   Listing assumptions can be limiting

WORKSHEETS (at the end of the chapter)

Worksheet N   Vision Statement
Worksheet O   Mission Statement
Worksheet P   Identifying Values, Staff
Worksheet Q   Identifying Values, Members

PLANNING PROCESS

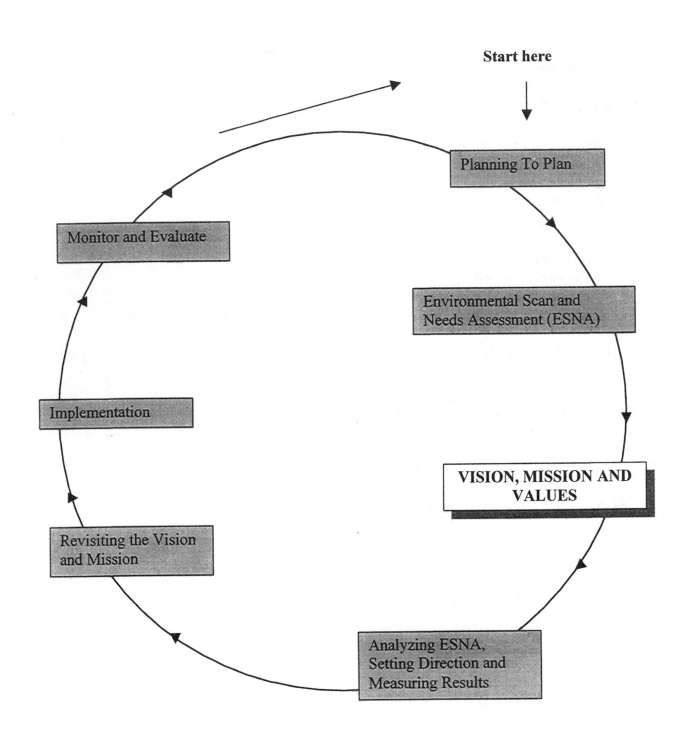

Start here

Planning To Plan

Environmental Scan and
Needs Assessment (ESNA)

VISION, MISSION AND
VALUES

Analyzing ESNA,
Setting Direction and
Measuring Results

Revisiting the Vision
and Mission

Implementation

Monitor and Evaluate

PHASE III
VISION, MISSION, AND VALUES

"Even if you're on the right track, you'll get run over if you just sit there."

Unknown

INTRODUCTION

Where we are: ESNA teams have been established and are gathering data. The planning team develops the draft MLC vision, mission, and values while the ESNA teams are at work.

Most library organizations are familiar with and have written mission statements that attempt to describe their purpose for being. Vision statements are newer to the field and are sometimes intertwined within the mission statement. Organizational values are even scarcer and frequently remain an option rather than a needed element in the planning literature. Definitions of and distinctions between vision and mission are explored first, followed by examples and a discussion of how to write the statements. Values and organizational philosophy are tackled last. Work on the vision, mission, and values statements as a progression.

Vision is a description of the organization's preferred future--a better future and a description of member libraries as a result of MLC activity. The statement must paint a picture of where the organization and member libraries want to go and what it wants to be--the words bring images and pictures of hopes and dreams to mind. It describes what the organization and its member libraries could look like when it reaches its highest potential ten or more years from now.

Vision Statements use **future** tense such as, "will be," "seek to be," "to achieve," "strive."

Vision benefits:
- Members and staff of the cooperative can see the "big picture" and not be limited by their framework of day-to-day operations or current service offerings.
- By describing the future and the image of a successful organization functioning in new ways, the pathway can become clearer.
- Decision making may become more efficient as potential actions are tested against the vision.
- Conflict may be reduced if consensus has been achieved on a vision.
- The vision statement can provide motivation and inspiration to members and staff alike.

Mission states what business the organization is in that distinguishes it from other businesses, other service organizations. M.E.L. Jacobs in *Strategic Planning*(p.# 58) defines mission as a "broad definition of an institution and its focus, which should identify its sphere of influence, its clientele, and major activity focus." (Note that it is not a list of the various functions of the organization as can be seen in many of the early public library mission statements.)

Mission statements use **present** tense such as, "is," "are," "does," "provides," "encourages."

A mission outlines the organizational purpose while a vision describes how the organization should look when it is fully successful. John Bryson in *Strategic Planning for Public and Nonprofit Organizations*(p.#67) sets this distinction: "Mission, in other words, clarifies an organization's purpose, or *why* it should be doing what it does; vision clarifies *what* the organization should look like and *how* it should behave as it fulfills its mission."

Strategic Planning for Library Multitype Cooperatives: Samples and Examples lists some of the benefits in having vision(p.#35) and mission(p.#49) statements:

Mission benefits:
- A focus for the "business" of the organization that allows a course-setting framework for all strategies and activities
- A context for tying resource allocations to the critical strategies for meeting mission priorities
- A clear statement of the organization's purpose for potential partners and funding agencies
- A decision tool for program and project strategies

Values as defined in Webster's dictionary are "the social principles or standards held or accepted by an individual, class, society, etc." In the planning process, the statement(s) of values describes the principles, beliefs, standards or code of behaviors that guide the MLC. This is an opportunity to define what the MLC desires or strives for in its culture and dealings with staff, members, stakeholders, and partners.

Values benefits:
- A solid understanding of the underlying principle that guides the organization helps assure that selected service functions, chosen strategies, and potential partnerships are "right."
- Staff can decide whether they "fit" with this organization by whether they "believe" in and are committed to what the MLC does as well as **how** it does its work.
- Articulated values contribute to member and public confidence.

Assumptions are the caveats or givens that establish parameters for the plan. They are statements based on some commonly held "assumptions"(e.g., "funding will remain static," "the MLC geographic region is set for the next three years"). Assumptions are sometimes identified in the beginning of the planning process and sometimes identified as they come up during discussion. The MLC may choose to establish assumptions. The authors are not recommending the use of assumptions for the simple reason that they may "contain" thinking, that they may "keep you in the box." External factors and internal situations can and do change so rapidly that assumptions may be incorrect within the first year of the plan .

VISION STATEMENTS

Having a vision statement is not as essential to day-to-day business as having a mission statement, yet author Bryson states(p.#156) that it is "hard to imagine an organization surviving in the long run without some sort of a vision to inspire it." Visions guide our action toward a shared purpose. The vision serves as the beacon to help us see our way. For a direct service organization, the vision does one more very important thing: it lifts the organization's purpose to a higher level by stating how society will benefit, how the organization contributes net value to society, how people are better off for what has been achieved. This "greater purpose" could be a part of the MLC vision, along with what the MLC and its libraries dream.

The impact on society that a direct service organization vision provides is perhaps more difficult to conceive for the organization like the MLC that serves other organizations. At first view, the MLC focus would seem to be bound by member needs and mandates. However, beware of "in the box" thinking, of limiting the possibilities and restricting creative growth. Engaging in futuristic, proactive and "for the greater good" thinking can be of great use for the MLC and its members. A well-crafted vision of success is highly desirable, though not easily developed.

Exhibits

Perusing the examples in *Strategic Planning for Library Multitype Cooperatives: Samples & Examples* (pgs.#35-46), one can see a wide variance in the vision statements. They run the gamut from short slogans to covering a page, from statements of goals and values to challenges facing the field. Here are a few that come closest to the definition we provide. Notice that some statements reflect the future state of being as if it were now, i.e., using the present tense. Others use the future tense as we have described in the definition above that, we believe, makes it less apt to be confused with the mission statement. It is a matter of preference.

> "Enabling member libraries to provide universal access"
> *Southwest Area Multi-County Multi-type Interlibrary Exchange*

> "The vision of success for Region V is:
> * All users have improved access to information and reading materials
> * All libraries are effectively able to meet the information and reading needs of their patrons
> * All libraries belong, participate, and contribute their uniqueness"
> *Central Jersey Regional Library Cooperative*

> "SEFLIN will position SEFLIN libraries as major leaders in the information structure of Southeast Florida by working cooperatively with libraries, educational institutions, information agencies, area businesses and government agencies. SEFLIN will enable libraries to transcend political boundaries and empower people to receive the information they need when they need it. SEFLIN libraries will affirm the social value of libraries as key contributors to the community's social and economic well-being and quality of life. SEFLIN libraries will facilitate the joint use of technology to provide the residents of Southeast Florida with links to local, state, regional, and global information resources."
> *Southeast Florida Library Information Network*

"The Southeast Library System envisions a world where libraries and individuals have direct and equal access to the diverse resources needed for education, work, and leisure. Technological developments will continue to challenge us to help libraries keep pace with the changing role of our profession."
Southeast Nebraska Library System

These visions of success are very broad and global, serving as a beacon, and pointing the way. The benefit to people is directly stated or clearly implied. The vision is a collective one, i.e., for its members. This composition seems to work best for organizations whose primary function is "to serve those who serve the public," such as the MLC.

The organization that directly serves the people has an "easier" time of describing its future (though describing its purpose may be more difficult). Here is an example from a public library that demonstrates that the best of the vision statements work in tandem with the mission statement:

Vision
"Carroll County Public Library will: continue to serve the community by offering a broad range of service designed to foster the love of reading; be the essential contact for all Carroll County residents, agencies, and businesses in need of information; serve as a gateway to a dynamic global network of information sources; strive to locate and deliver information and resources efficiently, accurately, and in the format requested by our customers; and provide excellent customer service by a trained and committed staff."

Mission
"The mission of the Carroll County Public Library is to provide adults and children of Carroll County with information and resources that support both lifelong learning and lifelong enjoyment."

Succinct, short paragraph vision statements are not easy to achieve. Alternatives include: 1) a one page scenario that is like a video clip on what is taking place in the future better state; and, 2) a combination of the full "video clip" and a short inspirational statement that acts as a motto or slogan. Here are shortened examples:

Video clip scenario:

Two women are printing out full text articles on a health related subject at their neighborhood library from an MLC sponsored, group purchased database. A family is dialing into the MLC's union catalog and finding books they will borrow directly from the state university and the public library in the next town. A proud may is announcing a cooperative grant from the MLC that will digitize prize photos and documents for public access on the on-line database. A school media specialist and the MLC director are making a presentation to the school administrators on the school media center's achievement of state information literacy standards. An MLC staffer is consulting with a member library on the selection of ncw technology for the new building they are planning. A member library director shares with her board the substantial savings on books and online databases achieved through the MLC group access service. The MLC's board president is testifying before the legislature for an increase in funding for regional cooperatives. A regional medical librarian is answering an inquiry from a nursing student at the university through a specialized reference service agreement brokered by the MLC. An MLC trainer is coaching a group of librarians who are hand-on in a computer lab learning the latest technology and how to train their publics in how to use it.

The slogan:
"The Librarian's Consultant"

Writing a Vision of Success

The MLC clearly cannot describe a vision that relates only to one type of library, but a vision of what is going on in libraries **because** of the MLC might well be useful, e.g., *School children are using media center computers to access the local history collection at the college. A family at the public library is on the 'hotline' phone requesting travel materials from another library. A professor is expanding his course bibliography from several libraries in the region while at his home computer, etc.* From these pictures or video clips, the MLC can derive a vision paragraph, and /or find a slogan that describes what the MLC will be doing and what the member libraries will be doing. Use *Worksheet N, Vision Statement,* to develop a vision statement.

Suggested Process
The planning team should ultimately come up with the vision statement. However, a larger, more representative group could be included In the initial visions of the future. A vision and mission can be developed at two half-day meetings or one all-

> *A vision statement has been described as a gyroscope--while events, customers, stakeholders, and the market are constantly moving, the vision keeps us centered and connected with our common destination.*

day meeting. *Example 9, Vision and Mission Meeting,* gives instructions on developing a mission and vision. Finalizing vision and mission statements for the MLC takes place over time. With the vision, get enough people involved to "think out of the box" and begin to create initial "buy-in." Groups will develop several drafts that need to be melded into one. Have a two person team bring one or two composite drafts to the planning team. Send out the one or two resulting drafts for input and comment from MLC staff, member library representatives, and key stakeholders. After the goals and strategic directions have been developed, both the vision and mission will be revisited to be sure the new directions are reflected in the statements.

A vision statement has been described as a gyroscope--while events, customers, stakeholders, and the market are constantly moving, the vision keeps us centered and connected with our common destination. With so much to recommend it, try creating a vision statement for the MLC. Remember too, that actual deep-seated commitment to any vision can only emerge slowly over time. It must be marketed to MLC and member staffs, and to stakeholders and politicians. It must be communicated over and over and used in prioritizing and decision making.

MISSION STATEMENTS

The mission statements included in the companion volume, *Strategic Planning for Library Multitype Cooperatives: Sample & Examples,* vary almost as much as the vision statements do. They range from a short sentence to long lists, from broad statements of functions to lists of services and products. We have made comments on a selected few.

Exhibits

"Lakeland Library Cooperative strengthens member libraries in eight west Michigan counties by providing the means to share resources, services and expertise for the benefit of individuals and communities." (pg.#53)
[Good points: declarative statement without saying "our mission is," clear about who it serves; tries to describe what it provides and why, though these could be more specific]

The Southeast Florida Library Information Network, Inc (SEFLIN)... "our mission is to work cooperatively with our members and the community to promote the collection and sharing of library resources, to facilitate training, to increase public awareness, to provide leadership, to encourage the joint use of technology and to support activities that enhance an individual library's ability to meet the informational, educational and cultural needs of its primary users and Southeast Florida residents." (pg.#52)
[Good points: states value of working cooperatively; describes what it provides and why]

"PALINET is to assist staff of libraries and information centers to deliver high quality, cost-effective services to their users through the application of technologies that foster information access, resource sharing and interlibrary cooperation." (pg.#55)
[Good points: serves staff--not institutions--although which staff is not clear; the end user is clear; the reason for the kind of services it provides]

"The mission of AMIGOS is to:
Provide innovative information services,
Promote regional cooperation and resource-sharing, and
Support libraries as leaders in education and information services." (pg.#55)
[Good points: brief and memorable with the PPS; easily leads into goals and strategies]

In reviewing these mission statements and the one your MLC writes, it is helpful to ask key questions:
Who are we?--a question of identity; who/what is the organization?
What needs does it meet or what problems does it address?--the important purposes to be served
What makes it distinctive or unique?
Why is it doing what it does?

Writing a Mission Statement

As data collection is taking place through task teams and assigned staff, the planning team needs to work on the vision and mission statements. Look at any existing statement on the MLC's mission and compare it to others from similar organizations. If this is the first attempt at defining the MLC's purpose, share examples of mission statements with the group (from *Samples and Examples*), review the definition carefully, and review the distinction between a vision and a mission. The group brainstorms possible phrases that begin to describe the purpose of the MLC. Whether creating or revising a statement, ask these questions: Does it describe the uniqueness of the MLC? Does it state clearly who or what the MLC is, and not list what the MLC does?

Once the group has a good start at sentences and phrases, give the task to one or two people to do the needed word-smithing. It is important not to get stalled here; consensus will likely not be reached at this point. Bring a draft or two or three back to the group and leave it before them as they move into the needs assessment phase. Use *Worksheet O, Mission Statement,* to guide the effort. The group will look at the vision and mission drafts again and incorporate any new ideas or directions that turn up. A mission statement takes time to develop. Once the planning team has a statement they can live with, try it out on a few staff and member administrators. Before considering the mission final, give it a good test by asking "outsiders" if the statement tells them who the MLC is. Formal adoption of the mission statement should definitely be reached before the strategies are begun.

VALUES

Values, principles, core beliefs, philosophy--by whatever name, we are talking about the code of behavior that guides an organization. Few organizations articulate the principles that guide them, the behavior they aspire to. Yet a discussion about these fundamentals is usually enlightening. Administrators are often surprised when, in open discussion with staff, there is such a wide range of stated beliefs and that the assumed "guiding principle" is not among the top values listed.

Clarification of fundamental beliefs can be very useful. A solid understanding of the underlying principles that guide the organization helps assure that selected service functions, chosen strategies, and potential partnerships are "right." Staff can decide whether they "fit" with this organization because they "believe" in and are committed to what the MLC does as well as **how** it does its work. Articulated values contribute to member and public confidence.

While statements of values or philosophy do appear in the plans of libraries and cooperatives, there are far fewer of these than there are mission statements and even vision statements. In *Strategic Planning for Library Multitype Cooperatives: Sample and Examples*, the authors mention the interesting range of approaches to the articulation of values and that they found a blurring of distinction between the values and functions of the organization. This is not uncommon or surprising. Values discussions are convoluted and emotion laden. They can be frustrated by efforts to define and distinguish between the terms and values, beliefs, principles, philosophies. The important point is " reflecting upon" the culture, the core beliefs, and the articulation of the results no matter what they come to be called. Effort should be made, however, to not repeat the functions of the organization, i.e., what it does, but to concentrate on **how** the MLC behaves or wishes to behave.

Exhibits

Samples and Examples (page 26), shows value statements:

2. Few if any High Plains programs benefit every member, but each member does benefit in different ways from membership.

5. The use of technology as a tool is necessary for High Plains and every member library...but technology shouldn't eclipse the need for maintaining strong foundation services and practices.

8. The strength of the System lies in its ability to react quickly and unbureaucratically to local and regional needs and opportunities....

Excerpts from High Plains Regional Library Service System, Colorado

A. Quality
The SCSL endeavors to provide services of the highest quality.

B. Knowledge
The SCSL believes that a well-trained and knowledgeable staff is it greatest asset.

C. Freedom of Information
The SCSL believes freedom of expression is a fundamental right of a democratic society and supports the Library Bill of Rights and the Freedom to Read Statement.

D. Access to Information
The SCSL believes that all citizens regardless of their location or means should have access to library and information services.

E. Equitable Treatment
The SCSL provides services to its customers in a fair and unbiased manner.

South Carolina State Library

Certainly for a service organization, values must be customer focused and may cover everything from "customer service is our first priority," to use of adjectives about service as in "excellence" and "quality," to a description of the relationships with members and stakeholders.

Values must also reflect internal behavior and beliefs. It is strongly recommended that a statement about the worth, treatment, and development of the staff be among the values articulated. The Southeast Florida Library Information Network, Inc., begins to do this with the following statement among its listed values:

We are committed to providing our members with quality staff who have a broad range of experiences to support SEFLIN programs and member needs. Our staff work as a team, respect each other's work and fully participate in the decision making process.

Writing Value Statements

We have already said that values must be customer focused and also reflect internal beliefs. So how does the MLC decide on an articulated code of behavior? As with every planning effort, start with the people involved--conduct an "assessment of beliefs." Developing draft values can be done at the same time as the ESNA (environmental scan and needs assessment) and is a good assignment for a task team. What the team will seek out is what members, stakeholders, and staff want the MLC to aspire to. It is like the vision in that the values are there to strive toward. In other words, it is not necessarily an identification of the active code of behavior or the values that are in place (whether above board or in undercurrent). The values statement(s) is how the organization wants to be seen by others and how it wants to be guided.

The values task team might use a focus group approach to get a set of values that can then be shared with a wider audience for confirming, adding, or voting on to select those few values that epitomize the desired organization. It is important to reach as many staff as possible for input and reaction to the developing draft; these are the people who must live by the code of behavior. The MLC director may choose to "lead the way" by proposing (or declaring) one or two core beliefs or underlying values that she/he holds for the organization. Whatever the method the team selects for doing its task, it must pose questions to the selected people who represent a cross section of the MLC. Remember that with a focus group, the facilitator sets the stage and begins with broad questions funneling down to more specific ones. Make the questions conversationally natural even if grammatically incorrect. For example:

1. What are the most important values for a service organization?
2. What kind of an organization would you like to do business with?
3. What kind of an organization would you like to work in?
4. What do you want your MLC to believe in, to be guided by ?

Another way to begin identifying values is to have staff and selected members respond to questions individually and then share their thoughts in a group meeting. A collective list is developed and then the group discusses and votes on its favored values. Worksheets for MLC staff (*Worksheet P*) and members (*Worksheet Q*) are provided at the end of the chapter.

The values task team presents the draft values statement(s) to the planning team. The planning team decides whether to recommend they be published in the plan and forwards them to the MLC board for approval. This interim approval step by the board can allay problems down the road should the board want substantial changes. Furthermore, the approved values along with the draft vision and mission statements are excellent tools for planners in making decisions and setting directions.

Reflecting upon and articulating the MLC's philosophy, culture, and beliefs is a worthwhile endeavor whether or not they end up in the published plan. When deciding to include them or not, remember that stated values speak to the staff, members, and public of the heart and integrity of the organization.

The example shows one all day meeting--9:00 to 3:00--where both the MLC vision and mission are tackled. It is a full day with much to think about. It could be split into two half-day meetings. The advantage to the full day approach is that it is easier to keep the distinctions between vision and mission, as they are "up front" throughout the day.

Pre-meeting: Send out readings about visioning, likely technological advances, and the future of libraries. Ask attendees to jot down their thoughts on what libraries could be like in the next ten years and what the MLC might be doing to keep libraries viable and valued. Be sure there are representatives from all types of libraries and that they especially "vision" for their type of library. Have them bring their notes with them to the meeting,

AM Session   3+hours with break
Welcome and Introduction to the Day:
Conduct introductions as needed. Review the day's agenda, etc. Define vision and mission and ask the group to help identify the distinctions between them.

Visioning:

20/30 min.   Be creative in preparing the group e.g. quote predictions from famous people, play some "futuring" music such as 2001: a Space Odyssey. Give example of a future scenario, make up your own or use the example in this chapter.

20/30 min.   Ask participants to use their "homework" notes and write a scenario. Get them started by setting the tone and asking questions... "Think about, picture in your mind the year 20_ _ . What is happening in libraries? What is the MLC doing? What major accomplishments have taken place? Describe what you are seeing as if through a video camera." Individually, have them write down their view of what is taking place.

10 min.   Several participants share their video scenarios (read slowly!) with the whole group. Comment on commonalities, etc.

5 min.   Demonstrate how to extract concepts from the scenario in *Example 10, Developing a Vision Statement*, to turn into statements. With the example given earlier in this chapter, these are some of the concepts:
- savings from cooperative purchases and group access
- reciprocal borrowing
- MLC advocacy and support for libraries
- technology consulting and training
- direct visibility for the MLC
- member advocacy, especially for funds for the MLC

60+min.   Divide into 3 or 4 groups of 5 or 6 people. The participants are to discuss their video scenarios, extract the main concepts they want to consider in crafting a vision statement. Provide flipchart paper and colored markers, urge them to be creative and visual, and to post their statements on the walls in the main meeting room when finished.

20/30 min.   Small groups read their vision statements to the whole group.   Take a straw vote on the one the group favors most and capture why. A caution here, make it clear the final statement will be crafted from all the input--put together from the parts of the statements from the groups. Circle favorite phrases and common themes in all the groups statements.

5 min.   Wrap up this segment. Have participants turn in their video scenarios. Leave the drafts on one wall. Tell participants that a two person vision/mission drafting team will prepare new drafts for the planning team and will refer to the video scenarios. Review the input and comments process. (The drafting team is to do both vision and mission. The team might be the consultant and planning coordinator, the MLC director and planning coordinator, or the planning coordinator and planning team member.)

Break for Lunch

PM Session 2 hours plus break

Mission:
20 min.   Review the definition from the morning. With whole group, critique examples (see *Samples and Examples*) of missions and discuss pros and cons of the MLC's current mission statement.

30 min.   In small groups, use *Worksheet O, Mission Statement*, to draft statements. Have groups post them on flipchart paper on the wall.

10 min.   Participants "gallery walk" to read the statements.

20 min.   With whole group, list the commonalties and favorite phrases. Discuss strengths, weaknesses and possible missing concepts. Compare against the vision statements.

20 min.   Try writing a draft by the whole group. Don't get stymied--write down agreements and disagreements. Send draft to vision/mission drafting team with all the flipcharts.

15 min.   Wrap up and celebrate accomplishments and hard work. Review next steps in process including input and comments stages.

Preparing a vision statement from individual or collective scenarios is a multiple step process. These directions are for the MLC choosing to write a statement. The MLC preferring the scenario itself as its vision need not go through these steps.

Read and refer to the vision and mission meeting (*Example 9.*) Whether or not the vision is created in the manner designed in the vision and mission meeting, the process up to now works in this way:

> From **Scenarios**, extract **Concepts and Themes**, turn them into **Descriptive Sentences**. Combine the sentences into a **Vision Paragraph**.

The following example scenario appears as an example vision in *Phase III, Vision, Mission and Values* and the extracted concepts appear in the vision and mission meeting directions. They are repeated here so that they may be seen together and show what concepts might be extracted from a scenario. It is important to remember that this scenario example reflects a future public library and that the MLC scenarios must cover all the types of member libraries (and preferably reflect activities with which the MLC is involved).

Scenario:

> Two women are printing out full text articles on a health related subject at their neighborhood library from an MLC sponsored, group purchased database. A family is dialing into the MLC's union catalog and finding books they will borrow directly from the state university and the public library in the next town. A proud may is announcing a cooperative grant from the MLC that will digitize prize photos and documents for public access on the on-line database. A school media specialist and the MLC director are making a presentation to the school administrators on the school media center's achievement of state information literacy standards. An MLC staffer is consulting with a member library on the selection of new technology for the new building they are planning. A member library director shares with her board the substantial savings on books and online databases achieved through the MLC group access service. The MLC's board president is testifying before the legislature for an increase in funding for regional cooperatives. A regional medical librarian is answering an inquiry from a nursing student at the university through a specialized reference service agreement brokered by the MLC. An MLC trainer is coaching a group of librarians who are hand-on in a computer lab learning the latest technology and how to train their publics in how to use it.

Extracted Concepts:
- savings from cooperative purchases and group access
- reciprocal borrowing
- direct visibility for the MLC

- MLC advocacy and support for libraries
- technology consulting and training
- direct visibility for the MLC
- member advocacy, especially for funds for the MLC

The vision drafting team takes the initial efforts and prepares one or two draft Visions for the planning team. The drafting team needs the flipcharts and notes from the meeting (or whatever input activities were undertaken). These include:

- the list of concepts and themes and the scenarios from the participants who created their own visions;
- the resulting three or four visions created by the small groups on flipcharts; and
- the notes on the favorite vision and the favorite phrases and the circled common themes

The drafts are presented to the planning team to revise and react and come up with an "official" draft vision. It may be necessary for the vision drafting team to word-smith after the planning team does its job. Finally, the "official" draft vision is sent out for reaction from selected staff and board, member representatives, and key stakeholders. Suggestions are reviewed by the planning Team and incorporated. The vision should now be close to complete.

There is however, one more time to look at the vision, that is after setting the direction, once the goals and strategic directions have been identified. This is an essential review to see if the statement expresses the new directions for the MLC. The vision drafting team may have some more work to do if essential concepts are missing. The planning team finalizes the vision or forwards it to the board if official authorization is appropriate before the plan as a whole is approved.

1. Individuals write scenarios of a desired future for the MLC.
2. The group(s) discuss and extract the main concepts or themes from the groups' scenarios.

Concepts and themes

_____
_____
_____
_____
_____
_____
_____
_____
_____
_____
_____

3. Turn the concepts and themes into descriptive sentences.

Descriptive sentences

_____
_____
_____
_____
_____
_____
_____
_____
_____
_____
_____
_____
_____

4. Combine sentences into a vision paragraph. Different combinations may produce several vision paragraphs to be presented to the planning team.

Vision statements

1) _____
_____
_____
_____
_____
_____

2) _____
_____
_____
_____
_____
_____

3) _____
_____
_____
_____
_____
_____
_____

5. The planning team reacts and revises and decides on the preferred vision paragraph which becomes the selected DRAFT vision statement.
Selected draft vision

_____
_____
_____
_____
_____

6. Send out draft vision statement for reaction from key staff and members. Planning team revises and determines a final draft vision.
Final draft vision

_____
_____
_____
_____

7. After developing the goals/strategic directions and objectives/major strategies, review the final draft and revise as needed to reflect the decisions on directions for the MLC (or revise the directions).

8. Send the reviewed draft vision for board approval.

Think about who/what the MLC is, what needs it meets, or important purposes it serves and why the MLC is doing what it does. Jot down phrases in the boxes . Then take some time to put them together into a draft statement.

Who is served(members, non-members, community) **and the name of the MLC:**

What main products, broad services :

Why (to what end, what needs are being meet):

Draft Statement:

_____
_____
_____
_____
_____
_____
_____
_____
_____
_____
_____
_____
_____
_____
_____
_____
_____
_____

Thinking about. . .

A. **The customers of our members:**

   How do we believe they should be served?

   _____

   _____

   _____

B. **Our members as customers:**

   How do we believe we should serve/treat them?   work with them?

   _____

   _____

   How do we want them to think of us?   work with us?

   _____

   _____

   What do they value about our services?

   _____

   _____

C. **Ourselves as internal customers:**

   How do want to be valued/treated?

   _____

   _____

   How will we feel when we are successful?

   _____

   _____

   What kind of work environment do we want to be a part of ?

   _____

   _____

Overall, what do we want our organization to be guided by? what do we strive for?

   _____

   _____

   _____

What are the most important values for a service organization?

_____
_____
_____
_____
_____
_____
_____

What do I/we value about our MLC's services?

_____
_____
_____
_____
_____
_____

How do we want the MLC staff to work with/treat us?

_____
_____
_____
_____
_____
_____

What do we want our MLC to believe in?   be guided by?   to strive for?

_____
_____
_____
_____
_____
_____
_____
_____
_____
_____

WHAT IS IT?

This phase has three main foci: making sense of all the data gathered; deciding on strategic issues and major directions; and finally, determining the measures of progress.

WHY DO IT?

Once the ESNA is complete, information can be organized so that it can best be used in decision making. This is the heart of planning--deciding which issues the MLC needs to address. It is critical that measures of success be determined. Without them, the MLC will have difficulty determining progress and if resources are being used in the best way to help MLC members.

STEPS

1. ESNA teams report
2. Planning team discusses and identifies key ideas/issues/needs
3. Staff summarize planning team discussions
4. Planning team and staff identify strategic issues
5. Staff organize ESNA information into broad topic/function areas
6. Staff distribute information back to planning team
7. Planning team decides on plan format
8. Setting direction retreat is held to determine goals/strategic directions
9. Staff prepare first draft of plan

KEY IDEAS & CONCEPTS

♦ Information from ESNA teams must be organized and synthesized to be useful
♦ Criteria are applied to ESNA information and strategic issues are identified
♦ MLC services tend to fall into seven function areas
♦ MLC planners choose a plan format from two approaches: goals or strategic directions
♦ MLCs determine how they will know whether goals or strategic directions have been achieved

WORKSHEETS (at the end of chapter)

Worksheet R	Analysis of ESNA Information
Worksheet S	Criteria to be used in Evaluating ESNA
Worksheet T	Strategic Issues
Worksheet U	Organizing Key Ideas/Issues/Needs into Function Areas
Worksheet V	Goals/Strategic Directions
Worksheet W	Major Strategies/Measures of Success
Worksheet X	Measurable Objectives

PLANNING PROCESS

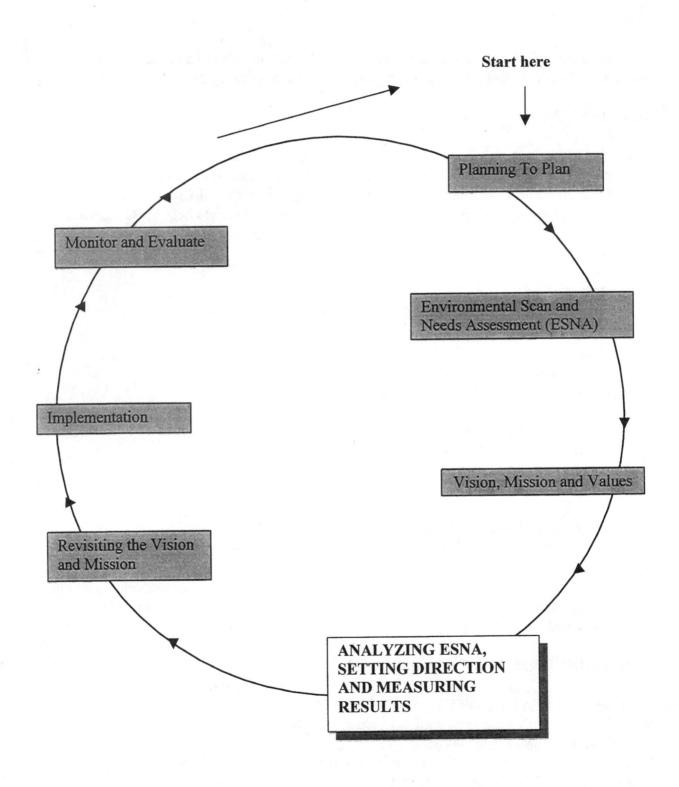

Start here

Planning To Plan

Monitor and Evaluate

Environmental Scan and
Needs Assessment (ESNA)

Implementation

Vision, Mission and Values

Revisiting the Vision
and Mission

**ANALYZING ESNA,
SETTING DIRECTION
AND MEASURING
RESULTS**

*"One reason things may not be going according to plan is......
there never was a plan."* Unknown

INTRODUCTION

There is a cartoon that shows a planning chart. On the left is a flow chart with boxes and lines and on the right is the same. In the middle is a cloud that says: "Here a miracle occurs." This phase in the planning process is like that cartoon.   Getting from the raw information to a coherent plan involves a thought process of taking large amounts of information, finding the most important pieces, and organizing them so the MLC knows what it wants to accomplish in the next three years.

There are three major tasks to be done through nine steps and they are described in this phase:

- making sense of the environmental scan and needs assessment information (ESNA)
- setting direction for the next three years
- establishing measures so the MLC knows when it has accomplished what it set out to do

Step 1:   ESNA Teams Report

As part of the ESNA process, ESNA teams have been appointed to implement a specific ESNA method or to investigate a major issue or topic previously identified. As the planning team meets, the ESNA teams will be reporting their findings.

Step 2:   Planning Teams Discuss and Identify Key Ideas/Issues/Needs

As the ESNA teams report, the planning team discusses the reports, applies previously determined criteria of importance using information from *Worksheet S, Criteria to be Used in Evaluating ESNA*, and identifies key ideas/issues/needs that the MLC might address in the future.

Step 3:   Staff Summarize Planning Team Discussion

Staff summarize the discussion after the planning team meetings on *Worksheet R: Analysis of ESNA Information*.

Step 4:   Identify Strategic Issues

Strategic issues can actually be identified in three places in the planning process. At the very beginning when the MLC board is writing the charge to the planning team, strategic issues may arise and be included in the charge. A second place is when the ESNA information is being reported to the planning team. At this point the planning team may identify strategic issues. Finally, at the Setting Direction Retreat, strategic issues may be identified. Strategic issues are mentioned here as Step 4 because this is the most likely place where they will arise. Regardless of when they arise, they can be described on *Worksheet T, Strategic Issues*.

97

Step 5:   Staff Organize ESNA Information into Broad Topic Areas

After the planning team has discussed the ESNA information, staff organize the key ideas/issues/needs by like topic under function areas using *Worksheet U: Organizing Key Ideas/Issues/Needs into Function Areas.*

Step 6:   Distribute Information Back to Planning Team

All of the summaries of key ideas/issues/needs from the ESNA reports and the organization into broad topic areas under functions are sent back to the planning team in preparation for a Setting Direction Retreat.

Step 7:   Decide on Plan Format

The staff with input from the planning team decide between the goals/objectives or the strategic direction/major strategies/measures of success approach to developing a plan so that this can be implemented at the Setting Direction Retreat.

Step 8:   Setting Direction Retreat

At the Setting Direction Retreat, planning team members and staff do the following:
- *   review ESNA summary of key ideas/issues/needs
- *   identify strategic issues
- *   select main goals/strategic directions
- *   develop objectives/major strategies/measures of success
- *   capture discussed actions for later inclusion in the plan

Step 9:   Prepare First Draft of the Plan

Staff take the results of the discussion at the Setting Direction Retreat and develop/massage this information into the first draft of the plan.

Below is a description of what is being implemented and when and how to implement the step.

MAKING SENSE OF THE ESNA

One of the most challenging aspects of planning is making sense of all the information gathered so that direction can be set by the planning team. The process of making sense is part factual, part rational, part strategic, and part intuitive. From all of the information that is gathered, the truly relevant and important pieces must be selected and organized into a structure that makes sense to the decision-makers, gives direction to members, board, and staff, and takes into consideration the strategic and service issues uncovered in ESNA.

There are two parts in this "making sense" process:
- organize information in a meaningful way
- determine criteria to use and apply criteria to the information to determine what is most important

Although analyzing the information and deciding/applying criteria are described separately below as if they were implemented linearly, in fact, they tend to be done at the same time.

Organizing Information in a Meaningful Way

What it is

Worksheet R, Analysis of ESNA Information provides a way to summarize the ESNA information into key ideas/issues/needs.   A separate form for each ESNA method should be used.

Setting Direction	Excerpt ANALYSIS OF ESNA INFORMATION	Worksheet R
ESNA Content	Key Ideas/Issues/Needs	
Statistics/Reports/Studies		

Example 11, Sample Analysis of ESNA Information shows what the ESNA methods might uncover. When actually completing a Worksheet each ESNA method would have its own *Worksheet R* since it is likely there will be more than one key idea/issue/need discovered. It is also quite likely that the same ideas/issues/needs may arise from different ESNA methods. This is a clear sign of something that should be addressed in some way.

Setting Direction	SAMPLE ANALYSIS OF ESNA INFORMATION	Example 11
Method	Key Ideas/Issues/Needs	
Statistics/reports/studies	Growing number of senior citizens	
Review of long-range plans	School plans show desire to offer more technology in SLMCs	
SWOT	State government becoming more conservative, threat to intellectual freedom	
Focus groups	Public/school libraries want access to academic libraries for their patrons	
Visioning exercise	Position libraries as major leaders in the information infrastructure	
Interviews	Local officials want their libraries to have more automation/Internet connections	
Surveys	Non-members want to join at reduced price for reduced services	
Membership forum	There is nothing about young adult (YA) service in the plan	
Legal Requirements	New state law requires all public entities to have staff Internet use policy	
Observation/intuition	New standards for education in state will threaten teachers and parents	

Establish and Apply Criteria

Whether a need is met or an key idea/issue addressed depends on the criticality of the need/issue and the ability of the MLC to respond. One method to use in determining this is to establish criteria against which needs/issues can be evaluated as well as the response capability of the MLC. *Example 12, Sample Criteria to be used in Evaluating ESNA* is adapted from the "Litmus Test for Strategic Issues" in Bryson's *Strategic Planning for Public and Non-Profit Agencies*. MLCs are encouraged to add their own pertinent criteria. Staff can present a shortened list of criteria to the planning team and with them decide on the five or six that will be used.

Setting Direction	SAMPLE CRITERIA TO BE USED TO EVALUATE ESNA	Example 12

Idea/Issue/Need_____

1. Was this issue mentioned by many people?
2. How often was it mentioned by different groups?
3. How many libraries are impacted?
4. How many types of libraries are impacted?
5. Does the MLC need to be proactive in this area? Reactive?
6. Would this be a major new thrust or maintenance?
7. Is this issue on the agenda of the state library? Library Association?
8. Is this issue on the agenda of the state legislature?
9. How great an impact can the MLC have on this issue/need?
10. How great an impact with the issue/need have on MLC members?
11. What is the financial risk in addressing this issue?
12. What is the opportunity in addressing this issue?
13. Will this require development of new service goals and programs?
14. How apparent is the best approach for issue resolution?
15. What are the probable consequences of not addressing this issue?
16. How sensitive or "charged" is the issue relative to community, social, political, religious, or cultural values?
17. What will be the impact on local libraries if the MLC takes this on?
18. Are there other organizations better suited to fill this need?

Depending on the criteria chosen, *Worksheet S, Criteria to be used in Evaluating ESNA* can be adapted to apply the criteria to any key ideas/issues/needs.

Setting Direction	Excerpt CRITERIA TO BE USED IN EVALUATING ESNA		Worksheet S
Criteria	Choices		Comments

When and How to Implement "Making Sense of ESNA"

It is at this stage that Steps 1, 2, and 3 are implemented:

Step 1:	ESNA Team Reports
Step 2:	Planning Team Discusses and Identifies Key Ideas/Issues/Needs
Step 3:	Staff Summarize Planning Team Discussion

ESNA teams were established to conduct specific ESNA methods or to investigate issues or topics of particular interest to the MLC. As the planning team meets, the ESNA teams will be scheduled to make reports about what they find. A major task of the planning team as they receive this information is to evaluate it and select from it the most important key ideas/issues/needs to be considered later as goals or strategic directions are developed. At meetings where the ESNA teams report, the selected criteria should be posted on flip chart paper so that the planning team has a clear understanding of how they will evaluate the ESNA reports. After each report, the planning team should be asked to apply the criteria and select the key ideas/issues/needs. This information can be posted on flip chart paper during the discussion. Following the meeting, the data coordinator, plan coordinator, or consultant (if there is one) can take the flip charts and summarize the discussion using *Worksheet R, Analysis of ESNA Information.*

SETTING DIRECTION

The approach to the planning process in this manual, as stated from the outset, is a combination of conventional and strategic planning. The combination becomes most apparent here in *Phase IV, Setting Direction.*

Where we are: the criteria have been applied to the information from the ESNA and the salient themes and important issues are listed. The task now is organizing these into useful categories and coming up with a readable, understandable document.

The standard organization is to develop a limited number of goals, each with its handful of objectives, and then brainstorm a long list of activities/actions to accomplish the objectives. The authors propose a new plan organizational structure that designates strategic issues, function areas, and then options for a goal approach or a strategic direction approach. Each of these is explained in detail below.

Strategic Issues	
Function Area	
Goals Measurable Objectives	Strategic Directions Major Strategies Measures
Actions	

Strategic Issues

What it is

The missing element in conventional planning is the **strategic** part of the ESNA analysis. There are often one, two, maybe as many as four issues or challenges that arise from the information gathered that seem so critical to the success of the MLC that they absolutely should not be lost. These issues may already have been identified early in the planning process and even included in the charge to the planning team. In the past these issues have been force fit into goal areas or, worse yet, subsumed as objectives or strategies, i.e., lost. We have, therefore, added the strategic issue. John Bryson in *Strategic Planning for Public and Non-Profit Organizations* deals with the strategic issue in great detail. We have adapted his model and added it to a revised long range planning model. The strategic issue is one that is so compelling it must be addressed. It is a true priority that means other goals or strategic directions may need to be postponed, down played or dropped in order to address the issue. Strategic issues may arise during the years of implementation of the plan. Tackling them as they come up, i.e., defining the issue and developing plans to address it as an update to the plan helps keep the plan viable and demonstrates the flexibility and opportunistic nature of the MLC.

The presentation of strategic issues in the plan has the following components:
> *Strategic Issue*--written as a question or statement that describes the challenge to the MLC (described in a page or less)
> *Why It's Strategic*--a full documentation of why it is a strategic issue, including citing the data and assessment source
> *Action to be Taken*--a discussion of the approach and selected actions to address the issue, whether it is a beginning step to be continued long term or a comprehensive multi-pronged campaign due to the immediacy of the challenge
> *Consequences*--what happens if the issue is not addressed?

Examples 16 and 17 show how strategic issues might be developed in two areas.

When and How to Do Strategic Issues

Step 4:   Identify Strategic Issues

Strategic issues can arise in at least three places in the planning process. They can arise so early that they are included in the charge to the planning team. They can surface directly out of the ESNA as a clear challenge for the MLC from the list of selected key ideas/issues/needs. As the planning team discusses the ESNA reports, strategic issues might be identified. Another opportunity will be at the Setting Direction Retreat when all of the ESNA information is reviewed. If identified early, staff can prepare *Worksheet T, Strategic Issues,* or these can be prepared at the retreat.

Function Areas

What they are

The function areas are the main services or functions of MLCs. Public libraries once defined roles; the new "revised planning process" speaks to service responses. In essence, the function areas are the typical broad service responses for MLCs. Research on multitype library cooperatives revealed a set of seven functions that are common among MLCs. However, it is expected that MLCs will revise the list of seven functions defined in this manual and add those unique functions or services that a particular MLC provides. The caution is to not break down the functions into very specific services, thus making a long list. The functions are used in this manual to organize the selected key ideas/issues/needs that resulted from the criteria being applied.

The authors acknowledge some creative tension between our Objective 1: to help MLC staff and boards think "outside the box" and the presentation of these seven functions. However, we believe these functions can be a helpful tool in accomplishing Objective 2: organizing information in a way that makes sense. MLC planners should not feel constrained to accept and organize their plan under these seven functions.

A short description of each of the seven functions is shown below. A full description of the functions is included in *Example 18* at the end of the chapter.

FUNCTIONS PROPOSED IN THIS MANUAL	
Library development:	Services that are delivered to the individual library to help it develop to best serve its clientele.
Communication:	Places the MLC at the center of the cooperative's information sharing.
Economies of scale:	Services that assist member libraries financially by allowing them to share costs.
Interlibrary lending and resource sharing:	Services include facilitating sharing information and resources among member libraries to benefit users.
Leadership and advocacy:	Calls on the MLC staff to be leaders and develop leadership in others.
Public access to resources:	Direct services to end users was in decline, but has reemerged as electronic services are developed at the MLC level.
MLC management:	Efficient and effective management of the MLC.

When and how to use functions

This is where steps 5 and 6 are implemented:

     Step 5   Staff organize ESNA information into broad topic areas
     Step 6   Staff distribute information back to the planning team

Functions are the organizing basis of the MLC plan. The key ideas/issues/needs are organized into broad topics on *Worksheet U, Organizing Key Ideas/Issues/Needs into Function Areas*. This can be done by staff alone or working in conjunction with a few members of the planning team.

This is often an intuitive process and requires looking at all the summaries of ESNA information, seeking commonalities and groupings that result in topics that should be addressed by the MLC. Each *Worksheet R, Analysis of the ESNA Information* and *Worksheet U, Organizing Key Ideas/Issues/Needs into Function Areas* should be sent to the planning team.

Goals/Strategic Directions, Objectives/Major Strategies/Measures of Success

Where we are: The staff and planning team have reviewed the ESNA information and identified select key ideas/issues/needs. These have been organized into broad function areas and presented to the planning team. Strategic issues have been identified and described. Now it's time to develop goals/strategic direction and decide what results are wanted.

What they are

There are two alternative approaches presented here for the organization of the plan. The first approach is to develop goals and objectives. The second approach is to develop strategic directions, major strategies, and measures of success. These two approaches are defined and explained below with examples of both approaches.

Goals/Strategic Directions--the broad statement of what the MLC is reaching toward/states the direction of intent

Objectives/Major Strategies--statements that further define the goal. Objectives are measurable, time bound results. Major strategies also delineate the goal but are not measurable; they are broad enough to require many strategies or actions to complete.

Rationale--why this goal/strategic direction was chosen. This could be a brief summary from the ESNA effort.

Measures of Success--used with major strategies when there is no measurable objective. It is the measure that the MLC will use to determine whether it has been successful. The MLC selects the level of measurement it is willing to undertake that is appropriate to each strategic direction.

Actions--the specific activities that make the objective or strategic direction happen. The meanings are synonymous here. Each action still requires many activities or steps to be accomplished, but this level of specificity is for unit or individual work plans

The **goals** are standard statements familiar to all of us. They are most useful when client-centered, i.e., stating what the client will receive or gain: *"Children of X area will receive increased services from MLC libraries."* It could also be written as: *"MLC member libraries will increase service to children."* In strategic planning they are called **strategic directions** and are written as action verbs that indicate a direction, e.g., increase, maintain, decrease, improve, expand, etc. It is client-directed: *"Broaden the variety of member services available to children."* The difference is not significant, it is more a matter of preference. (*Example 15*, at end of this chapter, is a comparison of the goals/strategic direction formats.) Use *Worksheet V* to develop goals/strategic directions in each function area.

Key ideas/issues/needs are collapsed and developed into goals or strategic directions. They should be broad enough so other objectives/major strategies can be grouped under them. This can be done at the Setting Direction Retreat.

Where we are: Once the initial goals/strategic directions are developed, then the objectives/major strategies are identified from the remaining key ideas/issues/needs.

Both the **objective** and the **major strategy**, in combination with others, will move the MLC toward the **goal** or **strategic direction**. An **objective** might read: "*By ___, ten MLC public libraries will provide programming for pre-schoolers.*" The major strategy would read: "*Provide enhanced services to pre-schoolers through member libraries.*" The difference is that the second is not measurable or as specific, allowing more possibilities in serving the target market. For those preferring greater specificity the objective may still be preferred--but make it measurable!

For most, the **objective** has been the bane of planning efforts. It is difficult to write so that it is a true objective, i.e. results oriented, measurable, and time-bound. It is frequently forced so that the measure may not be the best one and is often a guesstimate rather than a known achievable. Another pitfall is that measurable objectives are often written so that they actually measure activities rather than results. ("*Buy a computer by January, 1999.*")

Further, **objectives** have been written as specific actions that, if not achieved, mean failure. The classic example is "*To build a library branch in X community.*" If the branch is not funded, the effort does not succeed. Had the objective been written with a broader result in mind "*X community will receive library services,*" it would have allowed different strategies for achieving success. Perhaps the biggest problem with objectives is that too often they are not measurable as written. "*To improve services to pre-schoolers*" is not an objective.

The **major strategy** is not measurable. It is what it says it is, a major or encompassing strategy that takes many actions or strategies to complete. It is, therefore, easier to write. It starts with action verbs keeping it direct. For example, "*Define the basic services to be budget funded and identify services for which a fee would be charged.*" A major pitfall of this approach is when planners do not indicate measures of success.

Measures of success, borrowed from Total Quality Management, are used with major **strategies**. They allow for multiple measures and more options in deciding what will be considered success. As they are developed separately, both the measures and the directions can be simply and directly stated. There are four levels that apply to both measurers of success and measurable objectives.

Setting Direction	MEASURES OF SUCCESS/ OBJECTIVES LADDER	Example 13
Measurement Level	Example	Example
Measure *outcome* i.e. how well MLC meets needs OR impact on MLC members	Local library users will receive ILL requests in an average of four days as a result of direct ILL by member libraries	30 library users will report on how they used the Internet as a result of being trained by library staff
Measuring *output* i.e. MLC member action	20 MLC libraries will be able to complete ILL forms correctly	10 member libraries will conduct training sessions for library users following an MLC train the trainers session.

Measuring *client-centered inputs* i.e. the number of MLC members and staff served:
    - total number
    - total members
	20 MLC member library staff will attend a workshop on ILL direct loan requests	20 staff from member libraries will attend a train the trainers session on using the Internet

Measuring MLC *inputs* or actions (really measuring activities.) Not recommended.	The MLC will hold two workshops on ILL direct loan requests	The MLC will hold 5 train the trainers session teaching people to use the Internet

The MLC can decide which **strategic directions/major strategies** or **objectives** are to be measured at which level. The effort expended can vary greatly depending upon the importance and or "*measurability*" of the major strategy. Keep the **strategic direction** or **goal** in mind and ask "*How will we know if we've been successful?*" Do the same with the **major strategies** or **objectives**. Select the best measures that are most feasible. Always try to use measures at the top of the "ladder" first and then come down one step at a time until the "doable" level is determined. If the last two levels seem to be the most feasible for some of the **major strategies** or **objectives**, the **actions** or **strategies** will have to be decided upon in order to develop the measures. Do try to measure impact or outcome results at least for a few selected important efforts.

Worksheets W and *X* encourage the development of major strategies *(W)* with measures of success and measurable objectives *(X)*.

Here is an example of a function area/goal/objective:

Function:	Resource Sharing
Goals:	MLC members will have the capacity to use the Internet effectively
Objectives:	* 200 library users will learn to use the Internet from MLC trained librarians
	* 20 libraries will obtain Internet access by July, 1999, as a result of MLC member efforts
	* Staff in 20 libraries will be comfortable in using the Internet by July, 1999, as evidenced by their willingness to train patrons.

Here is an example of a function/strategic direction/major strategy/measures of success:

Function:	Resource Sharing
Strategic Direction:	Increase member libraries use of the Internet
Major Strategies:	1) Provide Internet access to members and their publics
	2) Keep staffs current on the Internet
	3) Seek technology funding
Measures of Success:	* Every member will have at least one public and one staff Internet access computer
	* Increase by X% the hits on the MLC's member libraries Web pages

Example 15 presents further comparisons of the two approaches.

The **actions** or **strategies** are the more specific activities to be undertaken to achieve the **objective/major strategy**: "*Train member library staff in services to pre-schoolers*," "*Hold 'partnering' meetings with pre schools, libraries and education officials*," "*Establish a pre-school and learning to read materials collection*." To the extent that **actions** can be decided upon during the planning process, include them in the plan. Where possible, indicate whether they are first, second, or third year efforts. It is strongly recommended that **actions** for the first year be identified and agreed upon and either included in the Plan or put into a separate implementation work plan. The ESNA and setting direction will generate solutions, actions, and ideas. It is what people do best and like the most. These **must** be captured along the way and brought to this phase and to implementation even though not all will be implemented. Much of the brainstorming on what the MLC will do has already taken place. The task here is to fill in the gaps and decide which are the most effective and feasible. If you recall in *Phase I: Planning to Plan*, in the Outline of the Process there is an implementation meeting (item 11) scheduled where actions might be determined. This will be discussed more fully in *Phase VI: Implementation*.

When and how to develop goals/strategic directions

The planning team can work to develop the goals/strategic directions and measurable objectives/major strategies/measures of success at a Setting Direction Retreat. These are steps 7 and 8:

Step 7:	Decide on a plan format
Step 8:	Setting Direction Retreat

Before the retreat, the planning team and staff should decide the desired format of the plan. It will be necessary to have made this decision to guide the discussion at the retreat. This may change or be adapted as the objectives or major strategies are written. There are pros and cons with each approach. Whichever approach is chosen, the most important factor is continuing the discussion until some level of measurement is determined.

The primary discussion about goals/strategic directions, etc., can be made at an all-day Setting Direction Retreat.

9:00 am	Introductions, review agenda for the day, review approach to plan. The facilitator for the retreat should also explain the approach to measuring progress toward goals or strategic directions and explain *Worksheets W or X.*
9:30 - 10:30	Assign the planning team into two or three small groups based on the broad topic and function areas but have the group remain together while giving instructions. At least one staff member should be assigned to each team. Review ESNA summary sheets *R, Analysis of ESNA Information* and *U, Organizing Key-Ideas/Issues/Needs into Function Areas* that were sent in advance. This will give the participants an opportunity to ask final questions and take comments about the topics. By assigning the team into small groups prior to this discussion, small group members can listen for comments about their topic/function area. If strategic issues have not yet been identified, that can be done during this discussion and also assigned to a small group.
10:30 - 11:30	For each topic/function area, the small group develops goals/strategic directions. Under each goal/strategic direction, objectives or major strategies/measures of success should be developed using *Worksheets W or X.* The retreat facilitator should move among the small groups, assisting them to look at the broad goals/strategic directions and more specific objectives/major strategies. The facilitator can also assist the small groups in developing the measurement necessary for either objectives or measures of success. After an hour, the planning team should reconvene to review progress. This is a chance to make sure each team is approaching the topic in the same way.
11:30 - 12:30 pm	Lunch
12:30 - 1:30	Return to small groups and continue work on objectives or major strategies/measures of success.
1:30 - 3:30	The full planning team reconvenes and hears presentations from each of the small groups. The planning team should be reminded that they are expected to come to agreement on the final plan to recommend to the MLC board; thus, the facilitator will seek a sense of agreement about the direction being determined. If planning team members do not agree with the small group recommendations, they should indicate what changes would make the recommendations more acceptable to them.
3:30 - 4:00	Wrap-up and summary. Explain that the results of the discussion will be further developed by staff and a first draft of the plan will be presented at a subsequent meeting.

Most groups have difficulty actually developing measurable objectives or measures of success. The goal of the Setting Direction Retreat is to have enough substantive discussion and decisions from the planning team that the staff or consultant can take this discussion and turn it into a cogent plan.

Step 9: Prepare first draft of plan.

At the conclusion of the session, staff or consultant take all the work done by the planning team and create the first draft of the plan. Use *Example 15* to see what a completed plan might look like. Remember to include rationale. The rationale is a brief paragraph that provides justification for the chosen direction. The plan writer pulls this together from the ESNA and planning team discussion.

Setting Direction	COMPARISON OF GOALS/STRATEGIC DIRECTIONS FORMAT	Example 15
FUNCTION--LEADERSHIP AND ADVOCACY		
GOAL: MLC members will increase the capacity to serve preschool children.	STRATEGIC DIRECTION: Increase service to preschoolers through member library services.	
RATIONALE: Demographic studies show an increase in families with preschoolers moving into the area. Children's librarians ask for help in designing programs for preschoolers. Third grade reading scores in schools show the need for more preschool reading readiness programs. Day care workers currently receive little or no reading readiness skill training and are requesting assistance from the public library.		
OBJECTIVES. 1) 20 day care centers will be trained to help kids achieve reading readiness through partnerships with local public libraries. 1) 20 libraries will form partnerships with local pre-schools and train day-care workers to teach reading readiness skills 2) Kids participating in program will increase their reading scores in 3 months over kids who do not participate in the program.	MAJOR STRATEGIES: 1) Promote partnerships among libraries, education and community organizations 2) Market the need for library services to preschoolers 3) Establish a collection of preschool and reading readiness materials	
	MEASURES OF SUCCESS: • Determine number of preschoolers served now and identify potential increase among selected libraries • 6 more member libraries will partner to enhance services • 4 public libraries will increase titles in preschool collections by X%	
ACTIONS: * Recruit librarians willing to participate * Train them to seek partnerships, train day-care workers * Develop bibliography of useful materials for local libraries and pre-schools * Contract for design and implementation of pre- and post-tests.	ACTIONS: * Hold a 'partnership' forum with pre-schools, libraries and education officials * Conduct a training series on pre-school services for member staffs and partners * Spearhead a preschool services listserv; newsletter to market services	

FUNCTION--LIBRARY DEVELOPMENT

GOAL:	STRATEGIC DIRECTION:
MLC members will have consulting services available in the area of technology.	Broaden consulting services in technology

RATIONALE: Top request for both continuing education and consulting is in the area of technology. Librarians and trustees want to be kept up-to-date on cutting edge issues. Internet filtering is a particularly critical issue for all types of libraries.

OBJECTIVES:	MAJOR STRATEGIES:
1) Increase number of questions about technology by 25% and answer 95 % of them satisfactorily. 2) Initiate training on Internet filtering policies for public library trustees with 50% of public library boards participating	1) Provide staff with technological expertise 2) Educate governing boards, non-library administrators, and key stakeholders in hot Internet issues 3) Establish 'computer trouble-shooters' among member libraries 4) Promote the adoption of standard Internet access policies among member libraries
	MEASURES OF SUCCESS: ● Member libraries will indicate satisfaction with the enhanced technological consulting through a member satisfaction survey ● 50 more technological consulting interventions will be conducted within 18 months ● 15 member libraries will have representatives of their governing boards, non-library administrators, and key stakeholders up to date with hot Internet issues ● 60% of members will have regionally acceptable Internet filtering policies
ACTIONS: * Hire a new technology consultant * Publicize availability * Evaluate performance * Develop workshop on filtering * Include articles on filtering policies in MLC newsletter	ACTIONS: * Train consulting staff in Internet use and access troubleshooting * Train or hire a 'computer/Internet' expert to backup MLC consulting staff and member library trouble shooters * Conduct a conference for non-library stakeholders in hot Internet issues * Disseminate updates on Internet issues to members and non-library stakeholders

110

SETTING DIRECTION	ANALYSIS OF ESNA INFORMATION	WORKSHEET R
ESNA Method	Key Ideas/Issues/Needs	

SETTING DIRECTION	CRITERIA TO BE USED IN EVALUATING ESNA			WORKSHEET S
Criteria	Choices			Comments
1. Was this issue mentioned by many people?	Lots of people	Moderate	Few	
2. How often was it mentioned by different groups?	Came up often	Moderately often	Seldom	
3. How many libraries are impacted?	75%	50%	25%	
4. How many types of libraries are impacted?	Four types	Two or three types	One type	
5. Does the MLC need to be proactive in this area? Reactive?	Should be proactive	Moderate	Reactive	
6. Would this be a major new thrust or maintenance?	Major new thrust	Revise current activity	Continue current activity	
7. Is this issue on the agenda of the state library? Library Association?	Yes	Don't know	No	
8. Is this issue on the agenda of the state legislature?	Yes	Don't know	No	
9. How great an impact can the MLC have on this issue/need?	Heavy	Moderate	Minimal	
10. How great an impact with the issue/need have on MLC members?	Heavy	Moderate	Minimal	
11. What is the financial risk in addressing this issue?	Great	Moderate	Minimal	

SETTING DIRECTION	CRITERIA TO BE USED IN IN EVALUATING ESNA			WORKSHEET S cont.
Criteria	Choices			Comments
12. What is the opportunity in address this issue?	Great	Moderate	Minimal	
13. Will this require development of new service goals and programs?	Yes	Moderate	No	
14. How apparent is the best approach for issue resolution?	Obvious, ready to implement	Broad parameters /few details	Wide open	
15. What are the probable consequences of not addressing this issue?	Major long-term	Some member dissatis-faction	No one will care	
16. How sensitive or "charged" is the issue relative to community, social, political, religious, or cultural values?	Dynamite	Touchy	Benign	
17. What will be the impact on local libraries if the MLC takes this on?	Great	Will help some	Minimal	
18. Are there other organizations better suited to fill this need?	Many	Some	Few	

Challenge: Member libraries can obtain telecommunication discounts under new federal act.

Strategic Issue: Congress passed the Telecommunications Act of 1996 that included discounts for schools and libraries on telecommunication costs. This could have a major impact on the libraries in the Two Mountain MLC. A major barrier to Internet access for staff and the public is the cost of a 56k or T1 line into our rural area. The FCC has been deliberating for months on how the discounts will work. With each iteration of the FCC rules and pronouncements, the issue gets more complicated and frustrating. It is difficult for the MLC staff to keep abreast of all the minute interpretations. We are in the second year of our long-range plan and this is not in the plan at this point in time. The Two Mountain MLC needs to address this issue.

Why the issue is Strategic: Most of the libraries in the state (70%) are already connected to the Internet. Our libraries are falling behind. If we can get the discounts, our libraries may be able to serve as community or school hubs for Internet access, thus raising both the libraries' ability to serve and visibility as an important contributing community institution. The MLC is also eligible to apply for the discount and this could provide additional funds to Two Mountain MLC for other projects. The competition for the discounts is expected to be fierce and time is of the essence. We can't wait until the next long-range plan is due to include this. We need to deal with it now.

Potential Action to be Taken:
- Assign a staff member to become familiar with the issue and rules
- Participate in joint funding with other MLCs and the state to hire a consultant who specializes in the discounts and can train all of our libraries
- Consider applying on behalf of our members to save them the frustration
- Apply for our MLC in order save money on telecommunication costs so the funds can be used elsewhere.

Consequences of Not Acting: Libraries would receive limited assistance in obtaining the discounts and fall further behind the state.

<u>Challenge</u>: School Media Centers are being removed from state's school accreditation standards.

<u>Strategic Issue:</u> School library media Centers have been included in the state's rules and regulations for accreditation of school districts. While the language about school library media centers is minimal, the rules do require that there be at least a certified and endorsed media specialist as the media supervisor in all school districts. At a recent State Board of Education meeting, the revised rules eliminated the requirement for school library media centers entirely. SLMCs were not singled out, many other requirements were eliminated as well, but it would still free local school districts to reduce the investment in their school library media program.

<u>Why is it strategic?</u> We are already seeing a reduction of professional staff in many school districts. This is particularly true at the elementary school level where school libraries themselves are being eliminated in favor of computers. Even with the current requirement in the accreditation rules, many school districts combined their funds to hire one professional media specialist to supervise the media program in as many as 10 school districts, thus adhering to the letter, if not the spirit, of the law. The new rule will hit particularly hard in Two Mountain MLC because our school districts have low budgets, and even if they want to hire a professional media specialist, it's hard to attract one to our area. The state board will be making a decision in four months. We need to act now to help protect our media centers. All of this is happening at a time when state reading scores are down. We need to show the importance and benefit of media centers to reading skills and other curriculum areas.

<u>Potential actions to be taken:</u>
- Contact state board member for our area and ask that the requirement about school library media centers be kept in the accreditation rules
- Get other librarians and board members to call as well
- Plan and present workshop on advocacy for school library media specialists
- Initiate and implement a PR campaign about the value of school library media centers
- Ask state library to participate and take the lead statewide
- Offer presentations to school boards, superintendents' meetings, and teachers on the value of school library media centers

<u>Consequences of Not Acting</u>: If we cannot keep school media centers in the accreditation rules, many of our rural schools will loose their school media professionals, and possibly, the school media centers as well.

Strategic issue	
Why it is strategic:	
Action to be taken:	
Consequences of Not Acting:	

1.   Library Development

Services that are delivered to the individual library to help it develop to best serve its clientele. They include:

- Continuing education (CE) and staff development. It could include CE delivered by the MLC or scholarships to member library staff to attend a CE event sponsored by another organization. Includes efforts to design distance learning delivery mechanisms by audio, video, or computer.
- Consulting with member library staff, director, or governing authority on any topic raised or needed by the member library. Consulting can be by phone, letter, e-mail, or in person, but involves the MLC staff member providing individual advice or assistance to member libraries.
- Increasing member library's capacity to serve its users. This could include helping a library obtain an Internet connection or helping them weed their collection.

2.   Communication

Places the MLC at the center of the cooperative's information sharing:

- Formal information distribution such as through membership meetings, newsletters, and publications
- Informal information distribution such as electronic listservs or "circuit riding" where MLC staff carry news and information from one library to another as they interact with MLC members through phone, e-mail, or listservs.
-

3.   Economies of Scale

Services that assist member libraries financially by allowing them to share costs of:

- Materials through cooperative collection development
- Staff that serve multiple libraries such as in technology or special population services
- Technology through group database licensing or development
- Equipment through group purchase for member libraries or MLC purchase for central loan or repair
- Financial accounting or public relations so that the library doesn't have to provide those on its own

4.   Resource Sharing

Services include facilitating sharing information and resources among member libraries to benefit their users:

- Author/title/subject interlibrary loan and reference back-up
- Assistance to local libraries to add their bibliographic information to a regional, state, or national database through services such as cataloging or retrospective conversion

- Shared or networked computer systems that allow libraries and their users to locate needed materials in other libraries
- Courier or other delivery systems (such as fax) that help libraries physically receive materials from other libraries and return the materials when necessary
- Assistance in developing and maintaining reciprocal borrowing agreements among member libraries or across the state.

5. Leadership and Advocacy

Calls on the MLC staff to be leaders and develop leadership in others:
- Advocacy to local and regional stakeholders, funding bodies, and governing authorities about the importance of libraries, including testimony and preparing written materials
- Representing member library interests on state and national committees
- Participating actively in professional library associations
- Partnering to advocate for library concerns at the state level
- Meeting facilitation to help member libraries conduct useful and productive planning sessions
- Research and investigation in key and emerging issue areas
- Forming partnerships with other groups that benefit member libraries
- Staying abreast of emerging issues and trends

6. Public Access to Resources

Direct services to end users was in decline but has reemerged as electronic services are developed at the MLC level.
- Providing library service to unserved areas of the geographic area through books-by-mail or bookmobiles
- Organizing information for electronic access by the public through Web pages or free-nets
- Managing public electronic mail accounts

7. MLC Management

Efficient and effective management of the MLC:
- Hiring and development of MLC staff so they have the needed skills to serve members
- Managing the MLC budget so that sufficient funds are available for MLC services and proper accounting and reporting is done
- Ongoing planning and evaluation of MLC services
- Development of the MLC board so that its members are well informed, responsive to MLC member needs, and able to plan for the future

SETTING DIRECTION	ORGANIZING KEY IDEAS/ISSUES/NEEDS INTO FUNCTION AREAS	WORKSHEET U
Function Areas	**Key Ideas/Issues/Needs (under sub-topics)**	
Library Development		
Communication		
Economics of Scale		
Interlibrary Lending and Resource Sharing		
Leadership and advocacy		
Public Access to Resources		
MLC Management		
Other		

Function Area _____

Potential Goals/Strategic Directions

1. _____
_____
_____
_____

2. _____
_____
_____
_____

3. _____
_____
_____
_____

Function Area _____

Potential Goals/Strategic Directions

1. _____
_____
_____
_____

2. _____
_____
_____
_____

3. _____
_____
_____
_____

Strategic Direction _____

Major Strategies:

1.

2.

3.

How to develop Measures of Success

A.   How well will MLC activity meet client needs? What is the impact on the client or the client's users? (May require asking them)

B.   What action will the client take as a result of the MLC activity?

C.   How many MLC clients and staff will be served?

       Total numbers _____
       Total members _____

Goal: _____

_____

_____

Measurable Objectives:

1.

2

3.

Measurement (to be included in the objectives above):

A.   By (X date), MLC members of MLC services will report satisfaction with a specific MLC activity.

B.   By (X date), users of members libraries will _____

C.   By (X date), MLC members will use an MLC service at a specified level.

D.   By (X date) , _____ MLC member staff will participate in MLC activities.

E.   By (X date) , _____ member libraries will participate in MLC activities.

WHAT IS IT?

Time to take a last look at the draft vision and mission statements in light of the strategic issues and directions and revise them for specificity and/or emphasis. It is a chance to be sure the final statements reflect the future direction of the MLC.

WHY DO IT?

Having a draft vision and mission early in the planning process provides all those involved with the same focus. The vision stretches thinking and opens up new possibilities at the start of planning. The mission describes the parameters for the work of the MLC and is the underpinning of the plans be made.

KEY IDEAS & CONCEPTS

♦ Keep the draft vision and mission statements visible and "up front" throughout the process
♦ Revisit the drafts once the new directions based on the needs assessment and environmental scan have been formulated
♦ Align the statements with the intent and emphases of the goals/strategic directions
OR
♦ Revise the goals/strategic directions to reflect the desired vision and mission

PLANNING PROCESS

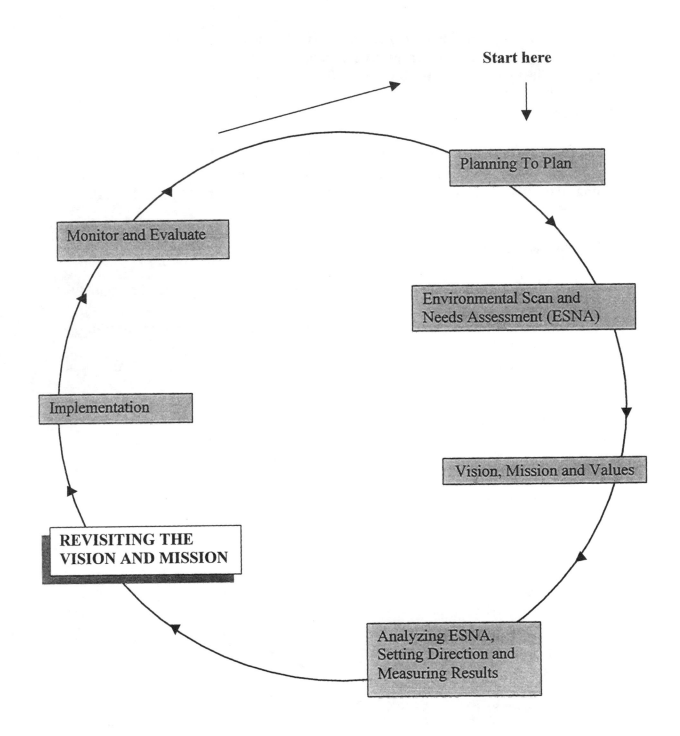

PHASE V
REVISITING THE VISION AND MISSION

"If everything seems to be going well, you have obviously overlooked something."
Unknown

It is at this point, when facilitating the planning process, that participants can be heard to say "We thought we'd finished all this--do we really have to go back and do it all over again!?!".. The answer is no... and yes. Unless there has been a complete change in the purpose and future direction of the MLC, all that is called for is a review. The review is conducted to be certain that the vision and mission adequately reflect the identified goals and strategic directions.

The next question is "then, why didn't we wait until now to develop the mission and vision?" Actually, this is an option and is suggested in some planning texts. In the experience of the authors, the process flows more naturally and is enhanced by drafting statements early on and then revisiting them.

Participants in the planning process can be frustrated when they are familiar with the organization's existing mission and vision statements and they are not dealt with from the beginning. Looking at the existing statements help to bring the MLC into perspective as well as put the planning team and all those involved on the same playing field.

The mission statement, which most libraries and library organizations already have, defines the purpose of the MLC, which is not likely to be completely altered in the planning process. Most mission statements are revised and improved upon during Phase III. Keeping the revised mission statement in front of different planning groups keeps them focused and aligned with the defined purposes of the MLC.

Vision statements are not yet prevalent in libraries and MLCs. Developing a vision early on kick-starts the planning process with an exciting view--a realistic ideal--of the future MLC. Whether or not a vision statement already exists, the visioning process is conducted. The process opens minds to new possibilities and educates those not familiar with the potentials of libraries to what the future could/should have in store.

A disadvantage to writing statements prior to the environmental scan and needs assessment is that very new and very different directions may be called for, thus requiring a greater effort when revisiting the drafts. This is not a likely occurrence for MLCs; indeed, it is not likely for most libraries. It can take place with non-profit groups that do change their purpose more frequently and with businesses in transition. One more caution: if the revisiting is bypassed and not done, the published vision and mission may not fully reflect the MLC's goals and directions.

What might cause a revision of a vision or mission statement? If the vision espouses the MLC being the gateway to the Internet and yet goals and strategic directions emphasize materials, collection development, and ILL, then this phrase must be revised. The vision might be vague:

e.g., *"The MLC is appreciated by its members"*; it could be improved with specific reasons for being appreciated: e.g., *"Anticipates and prepares libraries for future technology,"* or other specifics as determined in the needs assessment. The existing mission statement might try to cover all bases with *"the MLC helps libraries meet the informational, educational, and cultural needs of their users."* The ESNA could lead to more specificity with what makes the MLC unique: e.g., *"The MLC ensures the efficient use of regional, state and national resources among libraries,"* and so forth.

Dealing with revisions at this point usually involves improvements rather than major changes. The first example above, the gateway to the Internet, reflects an emphasis different from the goals and directions. This is an opportunity for the MLC to re-look at the strategic directions and determine whether the "gateway" really is an important role. Any number of reasons may explain this: perhaps the members have not anticipated this as a need, and the MLC should keep it in its vision, or it was a stated need but not captured adequately in setting directions, or a look at the needs assessment shows it overlooked the need. Whatever the reason, this revisiting gives the MLC a chance to re-look at their efforts, to consciously decide that this vision is what the MLC is about, and make revisions before the plan is completed.

Having defined the statements early on gives the planning groups a focus and a similar understanding of the purpose and hopes of the MLC. Revisiting the drafts allows for aligning, improving and time for input, reaction and buy-in.

WHAT IS IT?

What must be done to complete the plan, get it approved, and put it into action.

WHY DO IT?

Just as there is a *Planning to Plan Phase* there is a *Planning to Implement Phase*. Putting the final touches and blessings on the plan completes the document, however the process continues. There must be communication about the plan. The MLC staff need to have the first year's activities outlined and responsibilities assigned. The first year's work plan needs more specific costing and the next year's budget prepared. These are all sound business practices for businesses, non-profits, and MLCs.

STEPS

1. Finalize actions from *"Setting Direction, Phase IV"*
2. Develop implementation time line
3. Create MLC implementation plan and work plans
4. Get reaction to the plan and complete the final draft for board approval
5. Publish and market the plan
6. Develop an implementation budget

KEY IDEAS &CONCEPTS

♦ MLC staff develop the action plan
♦ Members, stakeholders, and staff react to the plan and provide input
♦ MLC director manages implementation with time lines and action plans
♦ MLC board, director, and staff sell the plan

WORKSHEETS (at end of chapter)

Worksheet Y-1	MLC Implementation Plan: Strategic Directions and Major Strategies
Worksheet Y-2	MLC Implementation Plan: Goals and Objectives
Worksheet Z	Individual/Team Work Plan

PLANNING PROCESS

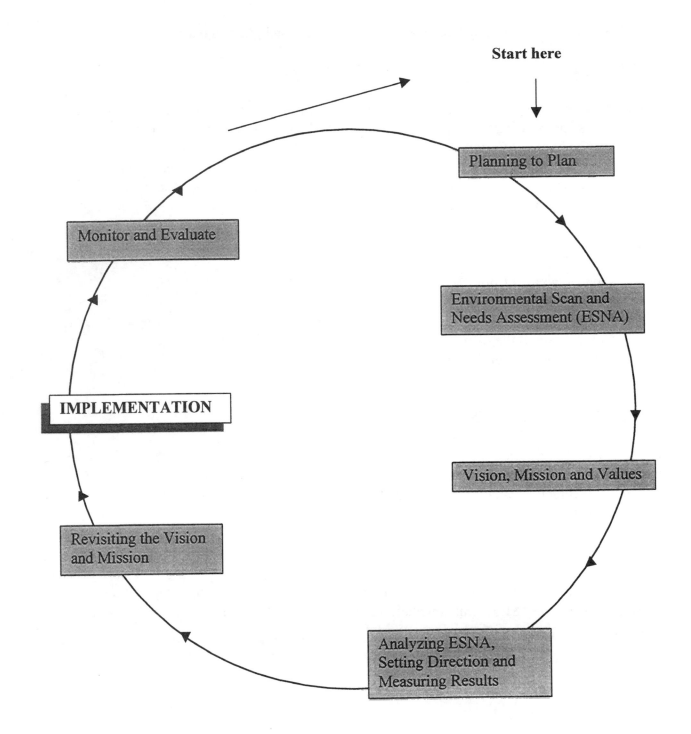

Start here

Planning to Plan

Environmental Scan and
Needs Assessment (ESNA)

Vision, Mission and Values

Analyzing ESNA,
Setting Direction and
Measuring Results

Revisiting the Vision
and Mission

IMPLEMENTATION

Monitor and Evaluate

"You give an order around here, and if you can figure out what happens to it after that, you're a better person than I am."

Harry S. Truman

FINALIZE ACTIONS FROM SETTING DIRECTION

In most planning experiences the planning team gets through objectives/major strategies, most of the measures of success, <u>and</u> making a hodge-podge list of possible actions. There are two options for developing the final actions. Up to this point, the actions have come from the ideas and solutions that have been captured from the different groups throughout the planning process. The planning team can choose to brainstorm further actions and then finalize them or it can request that the MLC staff come up with the recommended actions that the planning team would then approve and finalize. With either option, it is the people who have to do the work to implement the plan-- the MLC staff--who should have direct input on what must be done to accomplish the major strategies.

The MLC planning team may choose not to include the list of actions in the published plan. It may make the plan longer than desired, actions for every effort may not be easily determined at this time, or the board has delegated the decision to develop final actions to the MLC staff as part of implementation. Should selected actions not be part of the plan, it is strongly recommended that <u>sample</u> actions be included, clearly marked as suggested or sample. Suggested actions fill in the picture, helping to clarify the intent and possible initiatives to be undertaken. Whatever the decision, actions must be developed and are discussed here as part of the plan.

The planning team could turn over their draft plan to the MLC staff with the charge to identify suggested actions. Better yet, the planning team could hold an implementation meeting. The collective brainstorming that takes place during the meeting is much richer coming from the planning team which has been through the setting direction exercise, the MLC staff who will be doing the work, and the ESNA team chairs who are steeped in the needs assessment and data gathering.

The main purpose of the implementation meeting is to decide on recommended actions (the planning team and the board ultimately still have the decision authority). If the group is large, split into smaller groups, each working on a number of goals/strategic directions, then reporting back to the whole group. Be flexible; don't re-do what has been done, but if some newly suggested actions are better, use them. In most cases, what is needed is filling in gaps for some actions and augmenting others.

Actions

Review one goal/strategic direction at a time, the rationale, and then for each objective/major strategy look at the listed actions. Discuss the possibilities, seek more suggestions, then decide on those that are most feasible. Be sure to keep the ones that are not selected to use as guide posts for future sessions on implementing the plan. It is natural for the group to put the actions in sequential order, so just make it part of the assignment. Coming up with actions is a familiar and straightforward process; special tools or techniques are usually unnecessary. Deciding on which ones are the most viable comes through discussion and drawing on the group's experience. The desired result is a full set of actions for the first year of implementation and some potential actions for subsequent years. Be sure to put in the dates as they are identified.

Measures of Success

If the plan format uses the strategic model, i.e., major strategies and measures of success, there may be several that need completing. Remember the ladder for measures in *Setting Direction, Phase IV--the outcomes, outputs, client-centered inputs, inputs/actions*. Where measuring outcomes or outputs did not seem viable, the actions had to be determined so that they could be looked at for potential measures in order to evaluate success. Now is the time to complete these.

Look at some excerpted examples from the companion book in this Strategic Planning series, in *Samples and Examples.*

Exhibits

"Goal 1: Information Access
Through the network, end users will have the benefit of integrated statewide resource sharing systems by which to identify, access and retrieve needed information resources. . .
1.1: Support public access to the Internet and provide guidance in the use of the electronic superhighway.
1.2: Strengthen the interlibrary loan capabilities of member libraries in order that end users can secure needed information and resources not available at their local library. . .
1.6: Expand distance learning opportunities available to end users."
p. 130   Indiana State Library
[*Note the goal area, the stated goal, the list of very broad actions; some agencies label them as objectives; Indiana chose not to label them at all. These will require breaking down into more specific actions for implementation.*]

"GOAL II Promote, develop and support electronic access to information resources and on-line linkages for and among Region members.
OBJECTIVES
A.   Assure Access to a Freenet for Region Members.
        1. Identify the necessary requirements for providing access to a Freenet by the second quarter of 1995.
        2. Conduct a workshop for participating libraries on features of and hardware requirements for using a Freenet during the third quarter of 1996...
        3. Develop an evaluation by the fourth quarter of 1996...."
p. 96 Central Jersey Regional Library Cooperative

[The objective is not measurable, making it more like a major strategy (without the direction of increase, expand). Could include targeted number of people to participate. Actions are clear even though not labeled; they are also dated which makes developing a time line easy. Note that the evaluation is an action to be developed.]

"...Goal 5: To aid system libraries and media centers in providing enhanced service to children and youth through workshops and grants.
Objectives

    A. To increase by 50% the number of libraries providing special programming to children and youth. . .

        1) Presenting at least two workshops annually focusing on services to children and youth.

        2) Publishing lists of recommended materials in the newsletter.

        3) Providing four grants each year to system libraries for programs to children and youth."

p. 126 Meridian Library System

[The goal states how it will be accomplished, which seems appropriate for this two year plan, however, it does limit the options. The objective is measurable. They have put measures in the actions as well.]

Clearly the more consistent the structure for your goals/strategic directions, measurable objectives or major strategies with measures of success, and actions, the easier the plan is to read and follow. However, the best way is the way that comes most naturally whether or not the level of specificity is parallel or whether the actions are known at the time of writing--everything is not perfect in the real world! Absolutely crucial is giving a conscientious effort to include measures. If the initiative is too new to be well formed, indicate that evaluation will be defined as the major strategy comes more into focus. Libraries have been working for years to be more accountable; MLCs must do so to survive.

IMPLEMENTATION TIME LINE

> ***Preparing the master schedule or time line for implementation of the plan is a necessary and useful management tool.***

Preparing the master schedule or time line for implementation of the plan is a necessary and useful management tool. It is also a communication tool for members and stakeholders about the plan. Time lines are sometimes included in the published plan, but frequently, a more complete time line is shared with members after the plan is disseminated. This is as much a timing issue as it is a recommended practice--the time line takes some time to put together and is therefore done after the plan is published. It is very important to staff and of great interest to members. If a draft is possible, it should be prepared for their reaction when they are invited to react to the plan. If this is not possible or if it is decided that the MLC director is to put together the implementation time line, the staff should have direct input and it should be completed within one month of finishing the plan.

Tables, calendars, or a straight list are all good formats for the implementation time line. Including the dates/years for completing (or beginning and ending) major strategies has been encouraged because <u>now</u> is when planners can reap the benefits--all that is needed is formatting. On the other hand, when dates are not a part of developing the strategic directions/major strategies/actions, they must be determined as part of implementation. Another tip for managing implementation is to pull together all of year one by calendar month (as shown in one of the exhibits below) so that conflicts and over bookings can be readily spotted as the first year of the plan begins.

Three excerpted exhibits of time lines from *Samples and Examples* show different approaches.

Exhibit

July 1995
Employ a part-time technology consultant
Implement educational requirements for the use of the resource centers
Incorporate policies of responsibility for resource center use
Purchase a system car for administrator travel

August 1995
Union Catalog of Holdings
Choose most effective delivery system for ILL
Southeast Library System Handbook

Fall 1995
Reverence training
Technology showcase

December 1995
Subsidized access to online databases available...

Ongoing Activities
Internet, etc. training
Consultation activities
Technology purchase assistance to libraries. . .
p. 83 Southeast Nebraska Library System
[*The plan is for one year and can therefore be more detailed, and, as it is a plan limited to technology, it can be quite specific.*]

Exhibit

Goals/Obj./Activities/Tasks	Target Year/Years					Target Completion Date	Position/ Committee Responsible
	1996	1997	1998	1999	2000		
ELECTRONIC BIBLIOGRAPHIC ACCESS AND CONTROL:...							
1. Citizens will have prompt access to regional resources.	X	X	X	X	X	On-going	Exec. Director
a. Develop strategies for consolidating access to all regional bib. records and holdings.	X	X				December '97	Staff/Auto. Committee
b. Encourage end-user access to all regional bib. records and holdings	X	X	X	X	X	On-going	Staff/Auto. Committee
c. Provide libraries within the region with public access equipment at subsidized or no cost."	X	X	X			December '98	Staff/Auto. Committee

p.134 North County Reference and Research Resources Council

[Note that this time line includes a "who's responsible" column. The multi-year plans are by necessity more broad brush than the one year plans.]

Exhibit

Strategic Direction	Objectives	Year One	Year Two	Year Three
Provide high quality continuing education and training to member and associate member library staff	Offer 45-55 classes of Internet and related technology training classes to member and associate member staffs	Internet and ACLIN training	Communications training to meet as yet undetermined needs	Same as year two
	Offer 10-15 programs on a variety of library and management topics ...	8 classes on supervision; other to be determined	Classes to be determined by assessment of needs	To be determined"

p.142 Central Colorado Library System

[This is an excerpt from the time line for the whole plan.]

WORK PLANS

Writing down the steps to be taken to accomplish initiatives and assigned tasks is a common practice. The format of an action plan is the tool of choice; it is a simple way to organize and manage work. Work plans are a form of action plans. Staff can use work plans to organize their work as individuals and as teams (see *Worksheet AA, Individual/Team Work Plan*). The MLC director can use an annual or six-month work plan to assign and track the accomplishment of the actions and major strategies. Sample forms are given at the end of this chapter (*Worksheet Y-1, MLC Implementation Plan: Strategic Directions and Major Strategies and Worksheet Y-2, MLC Implementation Plan: Goals and Objectives*). Referring to *Worksheet Y-1 or -2*, note that it includes the measures of success and space for indicating what method will be used to actually measure the accomplishment, e.g., counting items/statistics, sending out a survey, taking sample counts of transactions at designated intervals, interviewing for feedback, conducting focus groups, etc. The MLC implementation plan and the staff's work plan have a column to fill in needed resources. With the staff, the actual resources given must obviously be discussed with the director. For the director, the resources column is the beginning of costing out the initiatives for developing a budget (discussed briefly in the last section of this chapter).

The benefits of using work plans cannot be overstated. The MLC director can review the time line and the work plan to track progress and manage the implementation of the plan. They are not only helpful to directors in the overall management of implementing the plan, but also as documentation for the board of the work to be accomplished or as the fodder for work reports and as the basis for performance review. They are helpful to managers in coaching staff and balancing the workload. They are helpful to staff (though sometimes seen initially as "bureaucratic paperwork") in thinking through the many steps or tasks needed to complete an assigned action. The combined action plan forms for each assignment become the individual's or team's complete work plan, serving as a picture of the entire workload. Work plans also make work expectations clear between staff and management, thus serving as objective tools for performance evaluation. We discuss work plans here as the best of the simple tools to use to ensure that the plan is effectively and efficiently implemented.

GETTING REACTION TO THE PLAN

Once the plan is drafted (including the actions that will be in the plan) and the time line is done, seek reaction to the document. Reaching this stage, the energy level is usually low and the time short. Don't give into the temptation to bypass seeking feedback reaction. Sending the plan out for a final review should not bring many surprises, only refinements and implementation questions. All during the planning process the staff, members, and key stakeholders have been asked for input and been kept informed. Still, the staff especially will be thinking "how does this affect me?" and members will be checking to see whether the services they want are included. If there is a major concern or a swell of

> *Sending the plan out for a final review should not bring many surprises, only refinements and implementation questions.*

opposition it can be dealt with, negotiated, and explained. Marketing the plan along the way helps get buy-in; getting reaction and feedback now tests and ensures the buy-in.

The most direct way to get reaction to the plan is to send out draft copies and ask for comments. Each staff member should have his/her own copy. Send copies to all those who worked on the plan and to key stakeholders. Have copies available at member libraries. Make it easy for the MLC constituents to provide feedback by returning their marked up copies, by sending in comments anonymously if they choose, or via e-mail. Hold an open meeting (or schedule several at different times and locations as appropriate) for in-person feedback. At the meeting the consultant or objective facilitator puts the plan into context, asks for overall reactions, and reviews and records comments on each goal, etc. Suggest that editing comments be handed in so that the meeting can be dedicated to content issues and questions. Be sure the feedback received is incorporated into the plan or reasons for not including it is provided later, and that questions are followed up with answers or responses. This is crucial--all the good will and support garnered to date could be lost right here.

The final draft. Reaction has been incorporated and word smithing done. The MLC board (or authorizing body) is given copies with the request for last chance comments. Again, the board has been brought along with the process so there should be no surprises. Should there be a controversial issue remaining, like a difference in opinion between the director and some of the members or staff, a meeting with the board will be necessary. Otherwise, the final draft becomes really final with the board's written feedback. The format is decided on and the document goes to publishing. Ahhh (big sigh)!

PUBLISH AND MARKET THE PLAN

Fit the message and the medium to the audience! Who is the main target group for the plan? Keep the target in mind when designing the format and finished product. If it is primarily a public document (i.e., for members, government officials, and the general public), photographs and fancy cover and formatting might be called for. If it is a working document for the board and staff, then a straightforward, but still readable (i.e., plenty of white space, side bars, etc.), document will suffice. There will likely be a handful of different audiences; some tailoring of the whole plan will help reach them successfully. Refer to the companion volume *Samples and Examples* on format, design and marketing for excerpts from system and state plans. Use executive summaries of the plan for politicians and non-library folk. Write concise briefs for the board that expand on the plan for really new initiatives. Package the vision separately and publicize the plan heavily. Share the implementation time line and the MLC Implementation plan with the board and funding bodies as appropriate.

Communicate! Communicate! Make personal presentations, attend member, board, and staff meetings, discuss the plan, its implementation, and evaluation. Create a videotape about the vision, mission, values and strategic directions, and major strategies. As with the planning process, send out periodic updates or report cards on progress, problems, successes, and changes. The vision, the plan, and related project papers should be a constant with staff at committee meetings and consultations. Prepare posters with planning themes, design individual cards with vision, mission, and goals.

> *Communicate! Communicate! Make personal presentations, attend member, board, and staff meetings, discuss the plan, its implementation, and evaluation.*

Use the formal communication network, as well as the grapevine; cultivate the messengers, woo the skeptics.

People must hear about the proposed changes, the implementation activities, many times and through many venues. They must understand what is happening or is about to happen, and be able to discuss it and explore the ramifications with others. Educational packets, workshops, and topic discussions on the listserv are ways to deal with big issues and initiatives. Build in milestones for long-term objectives, and celebrate interim accomplishments while moving toward the goal.

DEVELOP A BUDGET

The eight month to a year long process for writing a strategic long range plan means that a budget for the first year of implementation will most probably have to be submitted before the plan is finished. The MLC director will have to estimate the cost of the initiatives while the plan is being developed-- an uneasy prospect, but very real. Discuss the problem with the board or authorizing body as you begin the planning process. If the planning process was scheduled so that the plan could be funded in two different budget years, remember to include the cost in the projected budget. Once the plan is final, proceed with whatever cost analysis/ budgeting process is standard operating procedure. The information in the resource columns of the staff work plans and the MLC implementation plan is an excellent place to start looking at probable costs. As the budget is developed, it may be necessary to re-negotiate the resources that will be available to

staff to conduct their work. Indeed, it will be necessary to prioritize the major strategies and/or actions as there is never enough money to do it all right away.

The plans used in *Strategic Planning for Library Multitype Cooperatives: Samples and Examples* do not indicate priorities. Although some planning texts speak to the need for prioritizing, there really are not many examples of libraries with prioritized plans. There are lots of reasons for this, not the least of which is the inherent difficulty in prioritizing among all needed or essential services. It is also not always politically wise to make known what the board decides that it can and cannot do fiscally. Perhaps the most likely reason is that the board understands that priorities are established annually through the budgeting process.

It is certainly possible and worthwhile to set priorities for first-year and some second-year major strategies or actions. It is not effective or wise, however, to try to set priorities beyond this. The uncertainties and expected changes make it all but impossible. Whether or not the MLC chooses to publicize its priorities is a very individual decision based on the political, practical, and mandated realities. Two ways to establish priorities as part of the plan are:

1) indicating the year the major strategy or action will be undertaken, for example:
   a. now/year one
   b. next/year two or three
   c. future/years four plus;
   OR
2) indicating how they will be funded, for example:
   a. budgeted
   b. subsidized
   c. using 'extra' monies (grants etc.)
   d. desirable (if monies become available)

How to determine the priorities is also politically sensitive. To enhance trust and buy-in, the method chosen should be made known and done with the direct input of member representatives, not just done by the director or director and staff alone. The initiatives competing for priority placement could be weighed against a short list of imperative criteria. Refer back to *Setting Direction Phase IV* for using criteria in decision making and for an example list of criteria. "Criticality of need," "consequences if don't do it," and "political necessity" are three possibilities. Draw on the ESNA data and the collective professional judgement of those making the decision. Using criteria in a matrix is about as close to being objective as a subjective process can get.

All the management tools and techniques available to the MLC come into play in implementation. **But. . .** " whenever important opportunities to implement strategies and achieve objectives arise, they should be taken. In other words, it is important to be opportunistic as well as deliberate." John Bryson, *Strategic Planning for Public and Nonprofit Organizations* p. 37.

Remember the circle we used in the introduction of the manual to illustrate that the planning process is continuous? The final phase is titled *Monitor and Evaluate*.

IMPLEMENTATION   MLC IMPLEMENTATION PLAN   WORKSHEET Y-1
STRATEGIC DIRECTION & MAJOR STRATEGIES

Function: _____   **Strategic Direction:** _____

Major Strategy: _____

Measures of Success with method of evaluation: 1. _____

2. _____

3. _____

ACTIONS	TEAM/INDIVIDUAL RESPONSIBLE	RESOURCES start-up	ongoing	START DATE	END DATE	SPECIAL CONCERNS
1.						
2.						
3.						
4.						

138

IMPLEMENTATION   MLC IMPLEMENTATION PLAN   WORKSHEET Y-2
                          GOALS AND OBJECTIVES

Function: _____ Goal: _____
Objective: _____
Method of Evaluation: _____

ACTIONS	TEAM/INDIVIDUAL RESPONSIBLE	RESOURCES start-up ongoing	START DATE	END DATE	SPECIAL CONCERNS
1.					
2.					
3.					
4.					

139

IMPLEMENTATION   INDIVIDUAL/TEAM WORK PLAN   WORKSHEET Z

Function: _____ Strategic Direction/Goal: _____

Major Strategy/Objective: _____

Date: _____ Staff/Team Responsible: _____

ACTION (S)	STEPS	RESOURCES start-up	ongoing	START DATE	END DATE
	1.				
	2.				
	3.				

140

WHAT IS IT?

This is the last phase in our planning process. It involves assessing progress, measuring accomplishments, determining the impact of selected initiatives, and making course corrections.

WHY DO IT?

As stated in the companion volume, *Samples and Examples*, evaluation provides a number of benefits:
- an indication of the MLC's capacity to move in the desired strategic directions,
- objective look at the strategies in place and progress being made by the organization,
- validation of the MLC's successes in quantifiable measures,
- early data on emerging "next wave" of strategies to build upon developing trends and organizational strengths.

STEPS

1, Celebrate the completion of the plan
2. Evaluate the planning process itself
3. Monitor and evaluate
4. Reassess and develop the next MLC implementation plan

KEY IDEAS & CONCEPTS

- Thank the hard-working planners
- Document the good, the not so good, and the changes to be noted for a future process
- Evaluation asks "so what?"
- Evaluation comes directly from the measurable objectives or measures of success
- Check on progress every few months, reassess annually to write a new implementation plan

PLANNING PROCESS

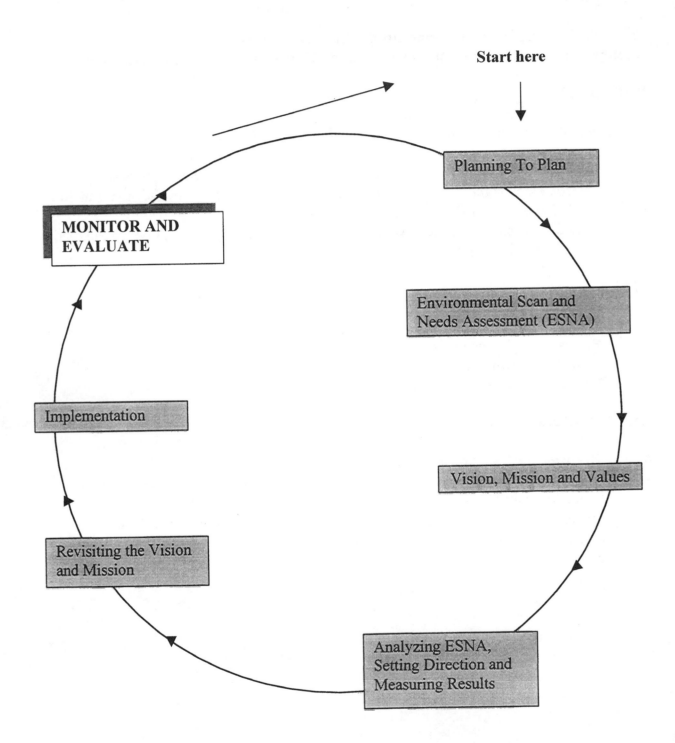

Start here

Planning To Plan

MONITOR AND
EVALUATE

Environmental Scan and
Needs Assessment (ESNA)

Implementation

Vision, Mission and Values

Revisiting the Vision
and Mission

Analyzing ESNA,
Setting Direction and
Measuring Results

"To keep progressing, we must learn, commit, and do - learn, commit, and do - learn, commit, and do again. . .on increasingly higher planes."
Stephen R. Covey

CELEBRATE

Its party time! The planning team and MLC staff and involved members and stakeholders have worked really hard and need to be properly thanked. Hold a reception celebration sponsored by the board. Give tokens of appreciation to all involved, with something special for the those who did the yeoman tasks. Recognize contributions with personal testimonies on how and what each gave to the project. Eat and be merry. . .it's well deserved!

DEBRIEF ON THE PLANNING PROCESS

Get feedback from all those involved in the project through a quick evaluation survey. Whenever possible, conduct an evaluative discussion with the planning team, the ESNA team chairs, and key staff. The MLC director, the planning coordinator, and one or two members of the planning team take the feedback, include their own perceptions, and write up a report on how the process went and what might be changed in the future. Specifically, seek responses to questions like these:

- What has been noteworthy or important to remember?
  e.g., consultant really helpful, but still took a lot of staff time; reduce project coordinators on-going job responsibilities during the planning process
- What could be added or subtracted to improve the process and result?
  e.g., give task teams another two weeks for data gathering; decide in advance what data will be used and keep it focused; include a one-page profile of the MLC and its members
- What might be done differently?
  e.g., provide the planning team with organized notebooks and help them keep them up to date to ensure all are on the same page and for easy referral; try to anticipate political hot potatoes (can't always be divined) such as a simple name change that can turn into a divisive struggle.

Evaluating the planning process itself is a useful endeavor and will be invaluable for future planning efforts. Don't forget to communicate highlights of the process evaluation. It says to people "we took our task seriously and planning is important enough to do right."

MONITOR AND EVALUATE

Purpose of Evaluation

The MLC that wishes to improve, grow, and remain vital needs to reflect on its successes and failures and seek continuous improvement. Evaluation is an integral part of planning; it is another phase on the planning circle. Among the reasons to conduct evaluations, there are three very basic ones:

- to monitor performance
- to make decisions about programs and services
- to give feedback to MLC staff and board

Monitoring performance

Determining whether the chosen actions and applied resources are moving the MLC toward reaching its objective is simply good business. It behooves key decision makers to pay regular attention to how the implementation is proceeding. We have suggested that a review be done every 3 to 6 months and a formal evaluation of progress be done annually when a new MLC implementation plan is written. This is, of course, in addition to the on-going day to day management of activities. Periodic reviews provide the opportunity to fix the problems that are bound to arise as actions are taken and the new initiatives are put into place. It is also very important to monitor changes in the environment and make course corrections. If circumstances warrant, take different actions than originally planned. And, don't forget that if some really critical challenge appears, deal with it as a strategic issue.

Making decisions

Implementation can become a kind of moving target; periodic review and evaluation ensures that what is working well and to advantage is maintained. The MLC director and staff will continually be making decisions to keep on target. Adjustments may need to be made in resource allocation or in the way a particular initiative is undertaken. The success of certain actions may mean dropping others that are not as effective. There will certainly be new opportunities appearing all the time as implementation gains momentum that will demand rethinking and changes in decisions.

Feedback

Knowing how well "we" are doing is essential to improved performance. The "we" is all those involved in implementing the plan and those responsible for the MLC. Information or feedback provides recognition as well as course correction which motivates individuals, work teams, or MLC committees. Seeing in statistics and anecdotal data the level of achievements provides the satisfaction that fuels renewal and growth. Demonstrating the worth and value of MLC services is the board's job and it is what ultimately keeps members and funding bodies on board.

Evaluating Results

While the scheduled "look see's" alert implementers to changes needed and keep the MLC on track, the more in-depth assessments are what evaluation is all about. They need not all be complicated or enormously time consuming (though measuring outcome can be resource intensive). Evaluation answers the questions: How has this helped achieve advantage for our members? and asks the what of "so what?" Evaluation provides proof of real value added for members and of increased member satisfaction. Indeed, if impact has been made and is documented, it can mean a substantial boost to the visibility of the MLC and, when properly marketed, leads to long-term recognition and long life. Another way to think about evaluation harks back to our opening pages: all the efforts put into planning mark where the MLC is going. The consequence of not doing evaluations is not ever really knowing if "you've arrived."

Concentrate on evaluating results of actions, not whether actions took place or not. Whether something took place or not is a result. Even how well it came off is limited to participant's or service recipient's feelings of satisfaction. For example, workshop evaluation sheets are helpful, but they are colloquially referred to as "happy sheets"--they do not measure results. Results are both outputs and outcomes. Outputs are the products, services, behaviors that resulted from the action taken--they are what's been done. Outcomes are the ramifications of what has been done, what difference it has made --the impact. Evaluation comes directly from the measurable objectives or the measures of success.

Look again at an excerpted goal and objective of one of the plans in *Samples and Examples* (the companion book in this series) that includes a measure:

"Goal 4: Library and media center personnel are well informed about system services.
    Objectives:
    ... B. To visit 85% of the library/media centers in the System every two years.

Visiting library/media centers is an action (not a true objective), the measure is 85%, and the time frame is every two years. This is a good performance measure; it should be easy for the responsible staff and management to determine whether it has been accomplished. The effort was clearly made to include a measure that can tell the MLC whether it is successful; it is an effort toward evaluation. What was the intended outcome of the visits? Was it worth the time of the MLC director? On the measures ladder, *Setting Direction, Phase IV*, it is the bottom rung, i.e., measuring an action. It is an input, not an output or outcome result.

Review of Measures Ladder	
Measuring Outcomes:	Local library users will receive ILL requests in an average of 4 days as a result of direct ILL by member libraries.
Measuring Outputs:	20 MLC libraries will be able to complete ILL forms correctly.
Measuring client centered) Inputs/Actions:	20 MLC member library staff will attend a workshop on ILL direct loan requests.
Measuring Inputs/ Actions:	The MLC will hold two workshops on ILL direct loan requests.

145

Had the MLC wanted to look at results, they would have started with the client and described what they would be gaining. The goal and measurable client-centered objective and actions might have been stated this way:

Example--Rephrased as GOAL and OBJECTIVE
GOAL:
> **Member and potential member libraries will make use of available MLC services**

OBJECTIVE:
> **75% of MLC library/media specialists will be well informed about MLC services within two years.**

ACTIONS:
> **Visit 3/4 of the centers in two years**
> **Prepare services brochure for library/media centers in year one, etc.**
> **Create a listserv**
> [The actions are also measurable; these immediately become the performance measures in the work plans of assigned staff.]

The EVALUATION METHOD might be:
> **Conduct an awareness survey in year two.**

Using the strategic format, the goal would be rewritten as a broader initiative allowing several major strategies relating to marketing services and indicating a direction for the MLC in increased use. The original goal statement, slightly altered, is really a major strategy --remember, major strategies are not meant to be measurable.

Example--Rephrased as STRATEGIC DIRECTION and MAJOR STRATEGY
STRATEGIC DIRECTION:
> **Increase use of available services by all MLC members and potential members**

MAJOR STRATEGY:
> **Promote MLC services especially to library/media centers**
[There would be additional major strategies that addressed increase use of services]

What might MEASURES OF SUCCESS be? Look first, and primarily, at the strategic direction and consider an outcome result:
> - **5 library/media centers will use, or increase use of, at least one more MLC service within two years**
> - **2 new members will join the MLC, etc.**

ACTIONS:
> **1. Visit 70 % of the library/media centers within the next two years**
> **2. Prepare services brochure targeting library/media specialists and schools**

Note that in the completed plan both examples would be under a function. In this case, it would be *Communication*. Also, there would be rationale statements between the objective or major strategy and actions. This would include data from the needs assessment that revealed low use of MLC services by a large number of library/media centers and a handful in the geographic area that were not even limited members

Refer to *Setting Direction, Phase IV,* for the authors' examples in the comparative tables. Under the goal area/function, goals and objectives appear next to strategic directions, major strategies and measures of success. Once objectives are made measurable (and preferably client-centered), the next step is to identify the evaluation method that will determine whether the objective has been met. With major strategies, measures of success are identified and then the evaluation methods can be determined. Examples of these are given in the tables as well. Evaluation methods can also be written as part of the objective or measure simply by stating "as measured by xxx," however, this can be grammatically challenging so it is not seen this way often.

Once objectives are made measurable (and preferably client-centered), the next step is to identify the evaluation method that will determine if the objective has been met. After major strategies, measures of success are identified and then the evaluation methods can be determined. The methods to be used for evaluating the objectives or measures can be included in the plan or can be included in the annual implementation plans instead. If done as part of implementation, work with staff who are assigned the initiatives early on so that methods are known from the beginning. Many measures simply require a current and future count or tally.

Typical methods of evaluation are surveys, keeping counts/statistics, observation, testing (pre and post especially), and anecdotal or testimonial information. The following are suggested methods of evaluation for some of the example objectives/major strategies and measures of success shown in the comparisons of the two approaches in *Setting Directions, Phase IV.*

Objective: *200 members will learn to use the Internet from MLC trained librarians.*
Method of evaluation: MLC trained librarians give brief evaluations to users, tally and report the number of users trained and the results of the user evaluations.

Measures of success: *Four public libraries will increase titles in preschool collections by x%.*
Method of evaluation: Count number of titles sent to the selected libraries and ask them to keep count of what they currently have and what they purchase.

Objective: *Kids participating in program will increase their reading scores in 3 months over kids who do not participate in the program.*
Method of evaluation: This is one that results in a true client-centered impact and is therefore more involved than just a tally or survey. Conduct pre- and post-tests (available or with help from the schools) on the control group, i.e., the participating preschool and one or two of the preschools not trained.

Measure of success: *Member libraries will indicate satisfaction with the enhanced technological consulting through a member satisfaction survey.*
Method of evaluation: The method is built into the measure.

As in the last example, evaluation methods can be written as part of the objective or measure by stating "as measured by." However this can frequently be grammatically challenging with the way objectives are written.

REASSESS, DEVELOP NEXT MLC IMPLEMENTATION PLAN

As year one of the plan ends, a more formal review takes place. The review is an evaluation of progress, a modest but astute/observational scan of the environment, an assessment of the previously identified member needs and any new needs that have surfaced. . . in other words, a quick reassessment of the MLC's direction and health. The reassessment becomes a planning session for year two. Actions are selected from the suggested actions list that was compiled during the development of the plan. New actions are added and decisions on what to implement are made. Adjustments are made to continuing actions. As circumstances dictate, a major strategy may need to be altered or dropped or added. Remember to communicate any significant changes made to the plan. Share results of the evaluations with members, stakeholders, and key decision makers.

By year three of the plan it should become clear that it is time for a new full-scale planning cycle to begin. If planning and evaluation and data gathering has been ongoing, the planning process should not be an arduous undertaking. Three years is considered today as the outer limit of a plan. Consider beginning a new cycle during the third year so that it is completed and implementation begun in year four. The transition from one cycle to another is not a stop and start event. Think of it as rounding that circle again, as illustrated in the introduction to the manual. Much will have been accomplished, some things will continue. Any major evaluation of impact should be completed and be begging for follow-up or innovation. New challenges should be on the horizon that will become strategic issues for the next plan.

The next plan. . .look at all we've learned. . .our next great plan will be easier!

KEYS TO A SUCCESSFUL PROCESS
adapted from John Bryson's
Strategic Planning for Public and Nonprofit Organizations

Strengthen leadership and assure adequate participation by stakeholders.
The MLC planning effort will need strong supporters throughout the process. Include major decision makers, managers, opinion leaders, and influential stakeholders.

Build understanding to support wise strategic thought and action.
Clearly communicate the purposes of the process (not just the resulting plan) to the board, staff, key member and community stakeholders. Engage them in the analyses and discussions required to build understanding of the decisions and choices being made; make sure there are no surprises. Manage expectations so that neither too much nor too little is expected from the process. Take the time and allocate the resources to "do it right."

Cultivate necessary political support.
The buy-in of top decision makers is usually crucial to the success of the planning effort. Buy-in is also essential from a large enough critical mass of staff and members that the strategic long-range plan will be supported and implemented.

Foster effective decision making and implementation.
Help the planners focus on the truly important issues. Link the plan to resource allocation and the budgeting cycle. Develop action plans in the implementation phase that will assure the achievement of major strategies and the realization of goals. Make these the operational plans and what drives the budget and resource allocation.

Design a process that is likely to succeed.
Build on existing successful planning, on well managed routines, and on useful change efforts, yet keep the strategic planning process open and exciting. Be realistic about the scope and scale of the planning agenda while still stretching for new gains. Try to find a balance that accommodates the day-to-day demands. Make sure that all involved see the process as genuinely helpful.

Manage the process effectively.
Commit the resources necessary for a successful effort. Seek help from people who are skilled in strategic planning.

BIBLIOGRAPHY

ASCLA. *Standards for Multi-type Library Organizations.* Chicago: American Library Association. 1990.

Baughman, Steven A., and Curry, Elizabeth A. *Strategic Planning for Library Multitpye Cooperatives: Samples and Examples.* Chicago: American Library Association. 1997.

Bryson, John M. *Strategic Planning for Public and Nonprofit Organizations.* (Revised Edition.) San Francisco: Jossey-Bass Publishers. 1995.

Bryson, John M. And Alston, Farnum K. *Creating and Implementing Your Strategic Plan, A Workbook for Public and Nonprofit Organizations.* San Francisco: Jossey-Bass Publishers. 1996.

Jacobs, M.E.L. *Strategic Planning: A How-To-Do-It Manual for Librarians.* New York: Neal-Schuman Publishers, 1990.

McClure, Charles R., et. al. *Planning and Role Setting for Public Libraries.* Chicago: American Library Association. 1987.

Nolan, Timothy M. *Applied Strategic Planning in a Library Setting, A Step-by-Step Guide.* San Diego: University Associates. 1987.

Public Library Association. *Planning for Results: A Library Transformation Kit.* Chicago: American Library Association. 1998

Waterman, Robert H. *The Renewal Factor.* New York: Bantam Books. 1987.

Zweizig, Douglas, et.al. *The TELL-IT Manual, The Complete Program for Evaluating Library Performance.* Chicago: American Library Association. 1996

SHORT CUTS TO THE PLANNING PROCESS

Yes, there are ways to cut corners and do just a piece of the process at a time. No, the shortcuts do not take the place of a comprehensive planning process that must be undertaken at some point. Institutionalizing planning, making it a natural and continuous part of managing the MLC means that doing phases of the process over time is perfectly appropriate. Here are some suggestions on "phasing in phases."

If Only a Vision Is Needed:
The MLC with a still viable plan it is following could conduct a vision/mission meeting as provided in Example 9, *Phase III, Vision, Mission, Values.* Prepare the visioning group with a futurist speaker, articles about cutting edge trends, plans and reports from other MLCs that open new vistas and possibilities. Use *Worksheet N, Vision Statement* to draft the vision. Review and revise the mission as needed, use *Worksheet O.* After the vision is finalized and approved, reconvene the group to take the visioning exercise one step further. This means having the group identify ways the MLC could bridge the gap between where it is now and where it would be while fulfilling the vision (see pgs. 152-153). The ideas are evaluated for feasibility and then turned into a new goal/strategic direction, or an objective/major strategy for an existing goal, or actions under existing major strategies. Should the vision point to a really new direction for the MLC that would be a radical departure from the current plan, move into the ESNA phase over the next 3 to 6 months and then on to the setting direction phase the following year. A new plan that addresses the new vision will soon be the result.

If There Is a Beginning or Emerging Business:
When most of the MLC plan is still viable but a specific service needs trouble shooting or the line of business is changing conduct a needs assessment in that area. Be sure to include in the needs assessment those issues/concerns that may seem peripheral but could impact on the main service. Choose a method to get at the current needs such as focus groups and/or selected member survey. Also choose a method that helps anticipate needs such as a literature search and other MLC or state agency plans or reports. It may turn out that the issue is now seen as a real challenge for the MLC, that it transcends the goals in the current plan and should be addressed as a strategic issue. Refer to the section on Setting Direction in *Phase IV, Analyzing ESNA, Setting Direction, and Measuring Results*, and use *Worksheet T, Strategic Issues.* If the findings do not point to a strategic issue then include it as an update to the plan.

If It's Time for an Environmental Scan:
Perhaps the MLC has done a thorough needs assessment but has not done an environmental scan. Conduct the environmental scan as described in *Phase II, ESNA*, using any of a number of methods. Do branch out beyond the board and standing committees so that fresh ideas and different perspectives are a part of the thinking. Again, a strategic issue may arise that is critical to the MLC so use *Worksheet T, Strategic Issues*, to help develop the issue. Otherwise incorporate the results into the existing plan as a new goal area, or under a current function, etc.

Note: Be sure to alert all involved of the changes and updates being made to the plan. To make it a living useful document, the plan must be used as a blueprint for the MLC's ongoing activities.

Analyzing a Vision Statement

Using the SEFLIN vision as an example, the planning team might analyze the vision statement in this manner:

SEFLIN Example	
Components of Vision Statement	**MLC Activities to Bring it About**
Position SEFLIN libraries as major leaders in the information structure of Southeast Florida	Continue SEFLIN Free-Net and training. Award community supporters of libraries.
Work cooperatively with libraries, educational institutions, information agencies, area businesses and government agencies	Sponsor teleconferences, continue community and library committees on SEFLIN projects, continue network of trainers.
Enable libraries to transcend political boundaries and empower people to receive the information they need when they need it.	Continue multitype library committees. Sponsor courier, serials union list, ARIEL and fax network, electronic virtual library service.
SEFLIN libraries will affirm the social value of libraries as key contributors to the community's social and economic well-being and quality of life.	Ask Free-Net users for impact stories. Share with legislators and decision-makers.
SEFLIN libraries will facilitate the joint use of technology to provide residents of Southeast Florida with links to local, state, regional, and global information.	Continue Free-Net with 7000 local Web pages and 6000 links.

Vision Analysis

Your Vision	MLC Activities to Bring it About